STRANGE and EERIE STORIES

PAT HANCOCK

Illustrations
by
ALLAN & DEBORAH DREW-BROOK-CORMACK

SCHOLASTIC INC.
New York Toronto London Auckland Sydney

Library of Congress information is available.

Produced by Somerville House Books Limited,
3080 Yonge St., Suite 5000,
Toronto, Ontario, Canada M4N 3N1

Series Editor: Dyanne Rivers
Educational Consultant: Valerie Taylor, York Region Board
of Education
Book design by V. John Lee Communication Graphics
Package design by M and Y Inc.

ISBN 0-590-20258-8
12 11 10 9 8 7 6 5 4 3 2 1
First Scholastic printing, May 1994
Printed in China

Contents

Rescue by Numbers

I can't believe I'm doing this, Pete thought as he peeled back the small plastic lid labeled Number 1. The oily smell hit him instantly.

At least they haven't dried out, he noted. He dipped the fine-tipped brush into the inky blue paint and stirred gently. Carefully, he wiped the excess on the edge of the little pot, then held the brush poised over the faint blue maze covering the white canvas.

"Looks like you got your way after all, Grandma," he muttered ruefully, steadying his hand.

He lowered the brush and filled in the first irregular shape marked with a tiny blue 1. As the color oozed past the outline, he realized he'd have to be careful about the amount of paint he applied. Doing this picture was going to take a long time.

But time is something I've got plenty of now, right? he told himself as he dabbed paint over another 1.

"And how did you spend your summer holidays, Pete?" he imagined Ms. Tompkins asking when he got back to school.

"Oh, doing a paint-by-numbers kit," he pictured himself answering. "It was loads of fun."

Pete grimaced, feeling sorry for himself. The pain in his right calf was down to a dull throb, not nearly as bad as it had been yesterday, but it still hurt a lot.

He wished he could take back that few moments yesterday afternoon.

If only he'd been content to stay inside the lodge's roped-off swimming area. If only he hadn't tried to show off by slipping under the rope and swimming out to the point. If only he'd paid attention as he climbed onto the slippery, moss-covered rocks, rather than trying to wave to the kids who'd stayed safely behind.

If only.... Maybe he wouldn't have slipped and opened up a sixteen-stitch gash in his leg. And maybe he'd be where he wanted to be today—white-water rafting.

His parents had offered to stay behind to keep him company, but he knew how much they'd been looking forward to the rafting. He'd been dreaming about it himself for the last two months.

So, he told them he'd be just fine in the cabin on his own and persuaded them to go without him.

Before they left, they'd stocked the fridge with plenty of pop and sandwiches.

"Just in case it hurts too much to go over to the cafeteria," Mom explained, adding two new bags of corn chips to the already impressive stash of junk food on the old wooden sideboard.

"And Mr. Kramer is just a call away," Dad added, pointing to the phone. "We checked with him earlier and he says he'll be happy to keep an eye on you."

"Dad, his office is right there," Pete said, pointing out the window. "Mr. Kramer could hear me from here even if I just whispered, okay?"

But, to humor Dad, he'd promised to phone the lodge owner. "Now get going. There's the van. I'll be fine. I'm not a baby anymore. Go."

Finally, they left. Pete waved from the doorway until the lodge van was out of sight.

Back inside the cabin, though, he couldn't settle. He felt restless. He tried reading for a while, but the Hardy Boys' latest adventure failed to grab him. He turned on the radio, but a man talking about home improvements was the only static-free show he could find.

It was when he reached over to turn off the radio that he spotted the box on the floor. His grandmother had handed it to him three days earlier, just as he and his folks were leaving for their vacation.

"Grandpa wants you to have this," she had said, holding it out. "It was his. He never got to work on it."

She'd paused for a moment, a faraway look in her eyes, then added, "The picture on top seems to have gone missing, but everything else is fine. Your grandpa loved doing these, you know. That's how he made the two pictures in my bedroom. Last night when I was looking at them, he told me you'd need this on your trip. Have fun with it—and bring me back a beautiful picture. I'll put it on my wall too."

"But I'll be way too busy, Grandma," Pete had protested lamely. "Maybe you should keep it here so it won't get wrecked."

But Grandma had insisted, and he had reluctantly packed the kit. He hadn't wanted to hurt her feelings by coming right out and saying that there was no way he was going to spend his holiday doing a paint-by-numbers.

Besides, since Grandma had come to live with them last year, he'd learned that there was no point in trying to make sense of some of the things she said about Grandpa. It worried him that she thought a dead person talked to her every now and then, but he knew how lonely she was. As Dad said, it was probably just her way of dealing with not having Grandpa with her anymore.

"The bonds of love are pretty strong," Dad had tried to explain, "especially after forty years. She still feels them, that's all."

Pete paused and looked at the canvas. He was surprised to see how many tiny spaces he'd filled in while his mind had been wandering.

Clearly, the dark blue made up much of the top section. Probably sky, he thought. Suddenly, he wished he had the picture that had originally been stuck to the top of the box. It would be nice to know what he was painting a picture of.

He decided to switch to another color. He was running out of places where he could rest his hand without touching a sticky blue spot. Obviously, oil paint took longer to dry than water colors.

Maybe I should let it dry a bit and come back to it later, he thought as he snapped the lid back on the Number 1 container. But as he wiped the brush on a paper towel, he was surprised to realize that he wanted to keep painting.

He studied the bottom of the canvas carefully and decided to open the green pot labeled Number 8. There were lots of little 8 shapes scattered across the lower third of the picture, and he could lean his hand on the table as he filled them in.

This time, Pete barely tapped the tip of the brush into the paint. This way, the brush kept its fine point and picked up just enough green to fill in a shape without oozing over the edge.

It crossed his mind that he was actually getting the knack of painting by numbers. The thought left him feeling both pleased and a little foolish— pleased because he was getting better at it, but foolish that he was getting any pleasure at all out of something so ridiculous. Try as he might, though, he couldn't talk himself out of doing it.

He'd been working for quite a while when the sound of heavy boots trudging up the front steps broke his concentration. He looked up to see Mr. Kramer poised to knock on the screen door.

"Hi, Mr. Kramer," he called and pushed himself away from the table. Only then did he realize how much his leg still hurt. He'd forgotten all about it while he was painting, but as he scrambled to stand up, a stab of pain shot up his thigh.

Despite the pain, he was determined to head off Mr. Kramer at the doorway. The last thing he wanted was for anyone to see what he was doing.

"Still hurting, eh?" Mr. Kramer commented as Pete limped toward him.

"Sort of," Pete answered, "but mostly when I walk on it, that's all."

"Well, your folks asked me to check on you, so here I am. How about I help you over to the dining hall for lunch?"

Lunch. Pete couldn't believe that it was lunch time already.

"Or maybe you'd like to come sit on the dock and do some fishing? What do you say to that?"

"Thanks a lot, Mr. Kramer, but I'm fine, really. I've got plenty to eat and stuff to read. I think I'd just as soon hang around here for now. Maybe I'll come down later this afternoon, okay?"

"Up to you, son. Just give me a shout if you need a hand."

"I will, I promise. Thanks again."

Pete watched as Mr. Kramer walked briskly back to his office. The noonday sun was dancing on the lake and many of the guests had retreated to the picnic tables tucked under the trees.

Why am I in here? Pete wondered. The answer that popped into his head left him feeling unsettled. Because I have to do the picture, he found himself thinking as he shuffled back to the table.

This thought bothered him and, when he looked down at the painting, he was even more disturbed. He hadn't realized how much of it was finished. He had only vague memories of opening the lighter green, rusty brown, black and pale blue pots, and didn't remember at all using the creamy white to top off what was obviously foaming, tumbling water.

Parts of the picture were actually starting to take shape, and they looked good. All the little sections were starting to fit together like the pieces of a puzzle. The effect was pretty impressive. But it was disturbing, too. The empty spaces seemed to cry out for the missing colors that would define them as trees, flowers, water, clouds or sky.

Pete was hungry—and tired. He realized his leg was throbbing. He wanted to take a break. But something stopped him. Something told him he had to finish the painting as quickly as possible.

His hand shook a little as he dipped the brush into a dark gray Number 12. Wondering what this color would reveal, he began to apply it methodically to the many small 12s on the left side of the picture. Rocks, he thought. They're rocks, poking out of the water.

"Hey, I get it," he announced. "It's rapids." Feeling pleased with himself, he began to work more quickly, eager to make sense of the unpainted sections along the shore of the racing river taking shape before him.

The faster Pete worked, the quicker the paint seemed to dry. He no longer had to worry about smearing it the way he had in the morning. And, once again, he was barely aware of the mechanics of what he was doing.

What he was noticing, however, in sharper and sharper detail, was how slivers of brown were actually parts of tall pines, dots of black were bark markings on spindly birches, and wedges of dark gray were weathered cedar shingles on a cabin tucked into the hillside. He had the growing sense that he was no longer filling in numbers but actually painting a picture.

For the first time, he checked his watch. Five o'clock. The day had disappeared. He wondered vaguely why his parents weren't back yet. Then he became aware that his head was aching. His throat was dry, too, and his fingers felt cramped and twisted. And in the background was the pulsing pain in his leg.

Pete began to worry about the gash. Maybe it was infected. The doctor had warned him to watch out for that. Maybe his throat was dry and his head ached because he had a fever, a fever caused by poison spreading through his body from the wound.

Then it hit him. There was a fever burning in him all right, but it wasn't caused by infection. It was a fever of fear. With a shiver, Pete suddenly realized that he was afraid of what lay in front of him. He was afraid of the picture.

His hand began to shake and his eyes blurred. He put down the brush and rubbed his eyes. Then he stared at the painting again. There was something hauntingly familiar about it.

He tried to focus on the scene. Slowly it dawned on him that he had seen this place before. But where? And what did it matter if he had?

Crazy as it seemed, he felt sure that it did matter. He had to recognize this place. Remembering that the pictures in Grandma's bedroom looked better if he wasn't too close to them, he pushed himself away from the table. Wincing in pain, he steadied himself against the sideboard and took another look at the painting. Think, he ordered himself. Think.

What he saw filled him with dread. He was almost certain that he was looking at a view of the river he and his parents had driven beside on Sunday. It was after they'd signed up for the white-water rafting. Dad had suggested that they take a drive along the winding road that followed the river's path, to get an idea of where they'd be going in three days' time.

They'd stopped several times to watch other rafters bobbing along in the churning, racing water. At one spot, Pete had noticed a small cabin flanked by four tall tamaracks.

That scene re-formed in his mind like a developing Polaroid picture. First, he recalled the cabin and the pines, then the cluster of white birches, the cedar shingles, the three large boulders at the river's edge, and the sharp bend just before the rapids. His memory offered up a snapshot that perfectly matched the painting.

His heart skipped a beat. Vague new fears tugged at the corners of his mind, pushing him to think the unthinkable—that the picture was waiting to reveal a terrible secret. A secret that was hidden in the only bare patch of canvas left to be filled in.

Pete sat back down at the table. His fingers felt weak and clumsy as he struggled to pry the lids off the last two unused containers—a fiery orange and a bright royal blue.

With a trembling hand, he stirred each color. Then he forced himself to dip the brush and apply orange to the four small shapes labeled 19. He wiped off the brush and held it over the blue pot. Then, one last time, he dipped the tip into the paint, and slowly filled in the two strips of blue dividing the small sections of orange.

With the last bit of blue in place, the secret was no more. Part of what Pete had thought was a log jutting out into the rapids could now be seen for what it was—the upper part of a body slumped over the log. The orange and blue life jacket outlined its shape clearly, as did the shadow of a leg trailing just under the surface of the water.

As a sickening certainty washed over Pete, Mr. Kramer pushed open the screen door. When Pete saw the look on his face, he knew that he was right—something terrible had happened.

"What's wrong? Tell me, please!" Pete shouted frantically. For a moment, the lodge owner looked confused as well as troubled.

"Tell me," Pete insisted, pushing himself up from the table. "Where are Mom and Dad?"

"Take it easy, son, or you'll open up those stitches," Mr. Kramer began, moving quickly to Pete's side. "Here, lean on me. Let's go sit down for a sec."

"I don't want to sit down," Pete said, his voice breaking. "I just want to know where Mom and Dad are."

"Your mom's safe, Pete. The state patrol just called. She'll be fine, so don't you worry about her."

"And my dad?"

Mr. Kramer spoke gently, "There's been an accident, son. Seems the raft capsized shooting the second set of rapids. Everything would have been fine if the tripper hadn't hit his head. But with him knocked out, people had to fend for themselves. They did well, though. Managed to get him to shore. But..."

Mr. Kramer paused to collect himself. He swallowed and took a deep breath, then went on.

"...but they couldn't find your dad, son. He's missing. Must have been swept down the river."

Pete began to shake.

"Listen to me, son. They're bringing in the helicopters right now. They should be here soon, and there's still at least two hours of light left. The other rafters are already searching. So, don't go thinking the worst just yet because..."

"But," Pete interrupted, "I know where he is!"

"Now, now, son. Listen to me..."

"No, you've got to listen to me. I know where he is. See." Pete held up the painting and pointed to the life jacket. "Look, just look."

Mr. Kramer leaned forward and peered at the picture.

"No," Pete ordered, "don't come too close. Here," he said, taking two steps back. "Now, look again."

Mr. Kramer stared. Suddenly, his eyes widened. "Why, that's the old Olliver place, down by Trout Bend. Where'd you get this?"

Pete was frantic. How could he possibly explain what had happened? It would take too long.

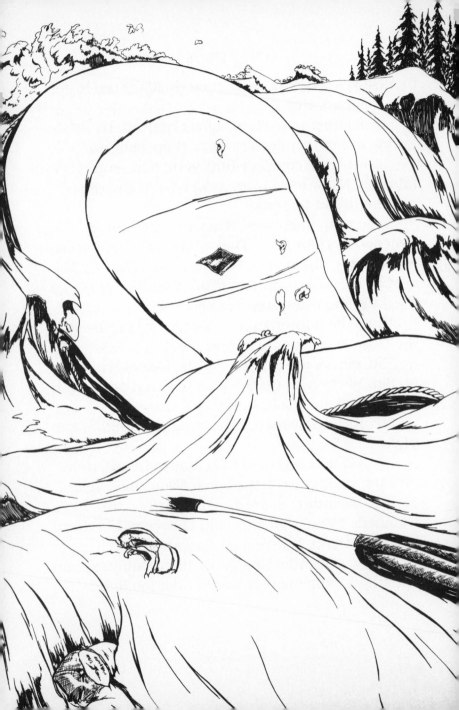

"That doesn't matter right now. Please, Mr. Kramer. I just know that's where Dad is. We've got to get to him."

"Well," Mr. Kramer began, "I'm not sure that this makes any sense, but...okay, it can't hurt to take a drive out to Trout Bend, if that'll make you feel better."

Pete stumbled toward the door. "Hurry, Mr. Kramer, hurry," he pleaded, pulling the lodge owner after him.

Fifteen minutes later, Mr. Kramer was dragging Pete's dad up the bank to where Pete sat, holding his leg. Pete had slipped scrambling down the hill toward the fiery orange life jacket they'd spotted from the truck, and his leg was bleeding again.

But he was feeling no pain. Since the moment Mr. Kramer shouted, "Your dad's breathing, son. He's breathing!" he had felt only incredible relief. That, and the urge to shout to the treetops, "I heard you too, Grandpa. I heard you."

The Raven

Cito would never admit it to most of his friends, but he actually liked hanging out at the library. It was better than being stuck at home with a babysitter while his mom went to night school.

For him, the library held happy memories of Saturday-morning story hours and puppet shows when he was little. And he always felt a thrill of anticipation when new arrivals showed up on the paperback racks.

One night, he found two new Gordon Korman books and another evening he discovered Daniel Pinkwater, who also came up with the kind of stories he loved to read. He even managed to catch up on his homework.

He liked the building, too. With its high ceilings, dark wood paneling and cushioned window seats, it reminded him of a movie mansion or castle.

Then the bird arrived—and ruined everything.

It was the first thing Cito noticed when he walked in that night. It sat perched on a tall pedestal to one side of the arched entrance to the children's section.

What's this? he wondered when he spotted it. A new security guard waiting to swoop down on book snatchers? When he got closer, though, he realized that the bird's swooping days had ended long ago.

It was big. And it looked even bigger mounted on the branch that served as a stand. Its ruffled black feathers had lost their sheen and its dull slate-gray toes ending in long curved claws looked dry and brittle. One of the stiff wing feathers was bent near the tip and poked out at an awkward angle. But the fine feathers covering the head were sleek and smooth and the slightly parted beak seemed poised to emit a screeching cry.

It was the beady yellow eyes, though, that bothered Cito the most. They seemed to glow with an eerie light all their own. He stared up at them as he sidled past and they stared back, cold and menacing.

Creepy, he thought, as he slipped into a chair and dropped his writing folder onto the table in front of him. He needed to come up with a third verse for a poem that was due the next day.

How about, "Crow, crow, go away. Stand in front of a Chevrolet?" he mused, stealing another peek at the sinister sentinel. He felt as if its eyes were following his every move.

Why don't you go read a book or something? he asked silently, and turned back to his work.

He sensed Miss O'Toole, the librarian, standing behind him even before she spoke.

"So, it's poetry tonight, is it?" she asked. Then she smiled and pointed at the bird, "I'm sure you'll write a great poem with him here."

Cito frowned. What on earth was she talking about?

"He helped a writer before, you know," Miss O'Toole added, "or at least we think he did. The research isn't complete yet, so we're not absolutely sure, but it looks like this is the same stuffed bird that once shared a room with Edgar Allan Poe. Mr. Herzig—he runs the antique store around the corner on Peckford—discovered it. When he suggested displaying it here, we were delighted."

Seeing the puzzled look on Cito's face, she paused. "You've heard of Poe?"

Cito suddenly recognized the name. "Oh yeah," he said. "Poe. He made horror movies, right? Like the one about the guy who accidentally buries his sister alive in a tomb in the house and she finally claws her way out. Then, when the guy sees her standing there all bloody and everything, he goes crazy and they both fall down dead and their mansion crashes down on top of them. He did that one, didn't he?"

Miss O'Toole was smiling. "That sounds a bit like 'The Fall of The House of Usher.'"

"Yeah, that's the one. The special effects are pretty good for an old movie. I've seen it twice...it's sort of scary, isn't it?"

"I'm sure it is. I haven't seen the movie. But I have read the story and I remember it very well. Edgar Allan Poe wrote it more than a hundred and fifty years ago."

"Uh oh," Cito felt foolish. "Then he couldn't have made the movie, huh?"

"No, but he did write some pretty scary stories that have been made into movies. I'm pretty sure there's a film version of 'The Pit and the Pendulum,' too."

"Oh yeah, that was gross," Cito blurted out excitedly. "It had all those rats and that ax swinging over the guy's head and the walls squishing in around him."

"So you do know Poe."

"Well, I've never read his books or anything."

"And you probably wouldn't like them too much just yet. The writing is very old-fashioned and they have lots of description, and you're more of an action story fan, aren't you?"

Cito nodded.

"But Poe wrote poetry as well," she added.

"That's funny," Cito chuckled.

Miss O'Toole caught on instantly and laughed too. "You're right, but most of his poems weren't funny—especially not the one about him." She pointed at the bird again.

No wonder, Cito thought as he looked up at the huge crow. There's nothing funny about him. He's horrible.

With its wings folded against its body and its head cocked to one side, the bird seemed to be listening to the conversation. For a moment, Cito was transfixed. He felt trapped in the evil glare glowing from the creature's cold, yellow eyes.

Miss O'Toole's voice broke the spell.

"The poem is about a man who's very sad and lonely because the love of his life, Lenore, has died. One night, he's all alone in his room. He hears knocks at the door and tapping sounds at the window, but nobody's there.

"Finally, he opens the window and a big black bird walks in and perches over his doorway. At first, the man's happy for the company. But then the bird starts to drive him crazy because it keeps saying the same word over and over."

Cito shuddered. He didn't want to hear any more. But Miss O'Toole kept talking.

"Mr. Herzig says that all the evidence he's collected so far shows that this is the same stuffed bird that came with the furnished room Poe was renting when he wrote the poem about Lenore. Looking at it all the time inspired him to write it. Isn't that exciting?"

Luckily, Cito didn't need to answer. At that moment, Mr. Leno came over from the reference desk to ask Miss O'Toole for help.

That night, the bird's menacing presence distracted Cito so much that he changed seats three times. No matter where he moved, it seemed to be watching him.

At one point, he deliberately sat with his back to it, but that just made things worse. Even when he couldn't see them, he felt the spying, prying yellow eyes boring into the back of his neck. No matter what he did, he couldn't shake off the eerie feeling that there was something unnatural about the bird, something that made his hair stand on end.

When Cito arrived at the library the next Tuesday, he headed straight for the cushions across from the aquarium. As he passed the bird, he kept his head turned away so he didn't have to look at it. He leaned back into the cushions and relaxed, watching the angel fish playing follow-the-leader though the elodea.

"Can't get me here," he whispered triumphantly. He opened his book and started reading.

But he had spoken too soon. When he looked up, a black reflection was shimmering on the glass of the aquarium. The beady eyes and parted beak were unmistakable.

Impossible, Cito thought. It's too far away, and the angle is all wrong. He closed his eyes, then looked again. The image of the bird was still there.

He scrambled off the cushions and made for the empty window seat on the other side of the room. Miss O'Toole raised a warning eyebrow when he banged into a chair on the way.

"Oops," he whispered. Out of the corner of his eye, he stole a quick glance at the bird and was relieved to see that its head was turned in the opposite direction. But his relief was short-lived.

Like someone who keeps bending a sprained finger hoping to find that it has stopped hurting, Cito kept checking on the raven. The next time he looked, he realized that he could see part of its right eye. Moments later, the whole eye was visible. When he looked again, he could see both eyes. Slowly but surely, the bird had turned its head. Its stare carried an unspoken threat that made his blood run cold.

He turned away quickly and blinked several times. When he looked back, the bird's wing tips were quivering and rising ever so slightly. It's trying to fly, he told himself. But it can't. It's dead.

The piercing shriek that followed was more than Cito could handle. He clapped his hands over his ears and crouched on the window seat, waiting to feel the talons he was sure were about to sink into his neck.

Instead, he felt a hand tugging at his arm and heard Miss O'Toole saying, "Don't be afraid. It's just the fire alarm. Stay calm and walk over to the door with me. Come on now. Let's go."

Cito struggled to his feet, feeling ridiculous. Then he smelled the smoke. He snatched up his knapsack and followed the librarian and the other kids she was herding toward the front door.

As he passed under the archway, he couldn't resist taking a last peek at the bird. What he saw stopped him in his tracks.

It was no longer staring at him. Its eyes were shifting from side to side, its wings were quivering, and its beak was opening and closing, as if it were trying to speak.

"Miss O'Toole, look," Cito croaked, pointing at the raven.

"What? Is someone else back there? Where?"

"There," Cito pointed.

"Oh Cito, this is no time to worry about the bird. Come on, let's go."

As Miss O'Toole nudged him toward the exit, he heard it—a low squawking sound. Again and again, all the way to the door, it echoed faintly above the din. It was the bird's voice, of that he was certain, and it kept squawking what sounded like one word—"Nevermore."

A month later, the library reopened. The fire had been a small one, confined to the area between the main desk and the arch. And although Cito was wary of returning, he'd had his fill of Mrs. Fonseca, the babysitter Mom had found. So, two days after the library opened its doors again, Cito was back.

When he walked in, the first thing he noticed was the new carpeting. The old oak counter that had served as the front desk was gone too. It had been replaced by a sleek white one that angled off on each side to form a U-shape.

And over near the archway on the right, where the pedestal had stood, was a large new revolving stand bulging with paperbacks. Cito scanned the rest of the main floor. The bird was nowhere to be seen.

He breathed a sigh of relief and headed for the big table. He sat down and dug out his history notebook, ready to study for a test the next day.

But try as he might, he couldn't concentrate. He found himself looking up every now and then as if to make sure the bird was really gone. Good riddance, he thought.

But he couldn't get it out of his mind. He could still see the piercing eyes, the shuddering wings, the gaping beak—and he could still hear the horrible squawk.

Miss O'Toole slipped into the chair beside him.

"The bird was lost in the fire," she said, as if reading his mind. "I felt terrible leaving it behind...and I felt even worse explaining what happened to Mr. Herzig. Luckily, he wasn't nearly as upset as I thought he would be."

"How come?" Cito asked.

"Well, it seems that the bird wasn't Poe's raven after all. Mr. Herzig was terribly disappointed. When all the evidence was added up, he realized he was wrong. Apparently, our bird was just somebody's worthless old stuffed crow."

Cito frowned. He wasn't so sure. "What if Mr. Herzig was right?" he began cautiously. "What if the evidence was wrong?"

Miss O'Toole smiled indulgently. "No, Cito. I'm afraid that's just wishful thinking."

As she stood up to leave, Cito suddenly knew what he had to do. He stopped her with a question.

"Wait. Can you show me where to find that poem you told me about?"

"Of, course. Come with me."

Cito followed her as she wound through the aisles in the main stacks.

"It should be in here," she said, pulling a fat book off the shelf. "Yes, here it is, 'The Raven.'"

Cito took the book back to his table, spread it open and began to read.

The first line wasn't too bad. "Once upon a midnight dreary, while I pondered, weak and weary" was easy enough to follow and it had a nice ring to it, too. But it was downhill after that.

Cito got the part about someone tapping at the chamber door and the bit about Lenore, but he had trouble making sense of the other long, rambling lines.

Frustrated, he turned the page. The raven finally showed up in the seventh verse.

He struggled on. "Ghastly and grim," it said. Poe had that right, he thought.

Then his heart skipped a beat. The word leaped out from the end of the next verse. He stared to make sure he was really seeing it.

Cito ran a shaky finger down the next two pages. There it was, at the end of every one of the next ten verses. The word the raven kept repeating—"Nevermore."

Cito stared as the words blurred and a vision swam before his eyes. His head was spinning. He saw a man sitting at a desk in a cold, dark room. The only light came from the flickering embers of a dying fire. The man was scribbling furiously, his eyes blazing with fear. A huge black bird mounted on a stand behind him was screeching one word—"Nevermore."

"Cito?"

Cito jumped.

"Sorry," said Miss O'Toole. "I didn't mean to startle you. I was just wondering if you found what you were looking for."

"Uh, yes, thanks," Cito mumbled, handing her the book. "I don't need this anymore."

Anymore. Nevermore. Poor Lenore. The words bounced around his head. Poor Poe, he thought, stuck in a room with that...thing!

And poor Mr. Herzig, he thought. But it's just as well he doesn't know that he had Poe's bird all along. He'd be so disappointed that it's gone. But I'm not, he thought, as he stood up to leave. I never want to see that bird again. Nevermore.

Bottom of the Ninth

Donny Adams wasn't just a fan. He was a believer. He didn't just cheer on his team, hoping they'd win. He believed they'd win—but only if he did his part, too.

It hadn't always been that way. When he was nine, Donny had been content to be a spectator. It had been fun to put on his new Condors cap and take in a few games with Dad.

They would munch their way through a big bag of peanuts, stand up every time the wave rolled by, cheer wildly whenever a Condor got a hit, and sing along with the crowd whenever the loudspeakers blared "Take Me Out to the Ball Game."

The next year was even better. For Donny's tenth birthday, Dad surprised him with tickets to five home games—the best seats in the stadium, behind home plate.

The Condors won all five games, doubling Donny's excitement and pleasure. He sat spellbound through each one, watching the players' every move and learning everything he could about them and the game itself. He wore his cap to each game and waved the copper-and-gold Condors pennant he'd bought with his own money.

Donny kept the pennant in a place of honor over his bed, beside the team picture he'd carefully cut out of the newspaper. And, whenever he could find the time, he watched his favorite team play on TV.

The Condors did well that year, finishing second in their division. But what was good for the Condors was bad for Donny. The next year, more fans bought season's tickets, making it harder to get good seats in advance. Ticket prices went up, too. That spring, Donny and Dad managed to take in four games, but they sat in the bleachers high above left field. When the Condors lost every one of these games, Donny told Dad he'd just as soon not go to Baylor Field anymore.

"It's not much fun sitting up in the nosebleeds," he'd explained. "You can't really see the game."

This was true, as far as it went. But Donny had another reason for not wanting to go, one he didn't share with Dad. The way he saw it, when he was sitting behind home plate, the Condors had won. When he sat in the bleachers, they lost. The least he could do was to stop bringing his team bad luck. He'd stay home for the rest of the season and cheer them on in front of the TV. If that helps them win, it'll be worth it, he decided.

But there were some days early that summer when Donny wondered if the price of a Condors' victory wasn't a little high. Gone was the fun of sitting with Dad among thousands of other fans, eating peanuts, smelling popcorn, doing the wave. Gone, too, were the many afternoons he might have spent tossing a ball, going to a movie or just goofing off with his friends. Whenever he had to choose between his friends and a ball game, he chose the game. After a while, his friends just stopped calling on him.

Once, he tried inviting some of them over to his house to watch a game with him. This had been his mother's idea. But Raoul had cheered for the Gators, Billy kept grabbing the remote and changing the channel to see how the wrestling was going, and Brad had teased him about arranging his pennant and the cards of the players in the Condors' starting line-up on the coffee table. The Gators won that afternoon, and Donny was pretty sure he knew why.

"They ruined everything," he complained to his mother later.

"Is that how you see it?" Mom had asked. "Maybe you should take a closer look at yourself," she added tersely, before leaving him alone to tidy up the living room.

What's with her? he wondered as he straightened the cushions and collected the empty pop cans. I didn't do anything. They just don't understand, and neither does she. Neither, he realized a week later, did his dad or his younger brother, Ian.

The next Thursday evening was picture-perfect, as only a late July evening could be. Mom was on the back porch stripping paint off an old kitchen chair, and Dad and Ian were off on a bike ride. Donny had turned down their invitation to go along. He had to get ready for the game.

"Come on. It'll be fun. We'll be back before dark," Dad had said. "The game can wait just this once, can't it?"

"Not for Donny, it can't," Ian piped up. "He's baseball crazy."

"Am not."

"Are so."

"Wrong. I just don't want to go anywhere with a snot-nosed little..."

"Stop it, you two," Mr. Adams interrupted, and hustled Ian out the door.

Good riddance, Donny thought, as he went upstairs to collect his good luck charms. He came back down wearing his Condors cap and carrying his pennant, a pile of trading cards and a poster of high-octane starter Billy Batista. The poster was a last-minute addition, but Batista had pitched a shutout the last time he'd gotten the call, so Donny felt sure having his poster out would bring him luck on the mound.

It was the bottom of the third inning when Dad and Ian returned to find Donny waving his pennant and shouting, "Yes. Yes. Yes!"

"So, I take it we're doing okay," Dad said, pushing aside Batista's poster so he could sit down on the couch beside Donny.

"Don't move...uh, I mean, could you please leave this here, Dad?" Donny asked nervously, propping the picture back against the cushion beside him.

Suddenly, he shouted, "Don't you dare, you little creep!"

Ian had been reaching toward one of the cards on the coffee table. He pulled back his hand as if stung.

"Sorrrrreee," Ian drawled. "I just wanted to read about Klein's numbers, that's all."

"They're not numbers, idiot," Donny lashed back. "They're stats. And you wouldn't understand them anyway. You don't know anything."

"That's enough, Donny," Dad interrupted icily.

"But, Dad, Klein wasn't up to bat yet," Donny rattled on defensively. "You can't touch his card when he's not up to bat. There, see what Ian did," he added, pointing to the television. "See? Klein just struck out. He brought him bad luck, right?"

"Ian didn't do that, Donny. But you did plenty. It's apology time, mister."

Feeling trapped, Donny mumbled grudgingly, "I'm sorry."

Dad sighed, "Now, fellas, what do you say we all sit down and enjoy the rest of this game?"

"Sounds good to me," Ian bounced over and snuggled up beside his father. Mr. Adams patted the space on his other side and said, "There's plenty of room here for you too, Donny."

But Donny didn't see it that way. It won't be any fun watching the game with you, he thought. You just don't understand. Nobody does.

Aloud, he said curtly, "Thanks, but no thanks." Then he picked up his cards, grabbed his poster and headed for the basement.

His mother opened the back door just as he reached the top of the stairs.

"Wait, Donny. What was all that shouting about?" she asked.

"Nothing," Donny grunted.

"Well, it was a pretty noisy nothing. And where are you going with all that stuff?"

"Downstairs, to watch the game on Grandpa's old TV. Or isn't that allowed?"

"Oh, it's allowed, but it doesn't sound like much fun. Where's your dad, and Ian?"

"In there," Donny said angrily, pointing to the living room. "They wrecked everything."

"Now where have I heard that before? Let me think," Mrs. Adams said. "Could it be someone named Donny who said it when...?"

She got no further.

"Can I go now?" Donny interrupted.

"Sure, but tell me, have I missed something here? I thought baseball was supposed to be fun. You don't seem to be having too much fun these days, Donny."

"Well, I will if I can get back to the game," he snapped, and started down the stairs.

Most of the basement was just that—a basement. But one corner had been set aside as a play area. There was a square of carpet on the floor, an old recliner and two lawn chairs to sit on, shelves for toys, a coffee table much the worse for wear, and the TV set Grandpa had left behind when he gave up his apartment and drove off to Florida in a new RV.

Donny switched on the TV and tuned in the game. He propped the Batista poster in front of the coffee table and flopped into the recliner. Leaning forward, he arranged his cards according to the starting line-up. He jammed his pennant into the space beside the chair's pop-up footrest, and settled back to watch. The way I want to, he thought. The way I have to, a faint voice whispered at the back of his mind. He quickly tuned this out and concentrated on the game.

With no one around to bother him, he was free to wave, cheer, hold up cards, cover his eyes, even stand on his head if that's what it took. This is great, he thought.

And, when the Condors came from behind to win in the ninth, he decided not to watch baseball upstairs again.

Before the next game, Donny headed for the basement to prepare. Remembering the winning formula he'd used on Thursday, he turned on the TV, propped up his posters—Green's as well as Batista's—positioned the chair, sat down, arranged the starting line-up, and jammed the pennant into place.

We're ready, he told himself. This is going to be fun. He checked his watch. Five minutes to go. It occurred to him that this was just enough time to make some popcorn.

Leaving his cap behind on the chair, he whipped upstairs, put a bag of popcorn into the microwave, set the timer and waited impatiently for the buzzer to sound.

Then he raced back downstairs, put his cap back on and settled into the recliner. "Let's play ball," he announced as the players took to the field. The Condors won handily.

Then, just when it looked as if the team and Donny were doing everything right and the Condors might actually take their division, things started going terribly wrong.

The team set out on a twelve-game road trip and lost five in a row. Desperately, Donny tinkered with his rules for bringing off a Condors' win until he could barely keep track of them. He became a boy possessed as the preparations before each game escalated into a frantic race to get everything done on time.

He was also worried that something he'd done had caused the string of defeats. Was the popcorn all gone when Batista loaded the bases and threw the lollipop that Feliciano had drilled high over the right-field wall? Should he eat it more slowly the next time, or should he forget it altogether? Maybe that would do the trick.

As the next game approached, Donny realized he was in trouble. His hands trembled as he opened the trunk and his eyes blurred as he tried to organize the Condors' cards into their starting line-up. I can't take it any more, he suddenly found himself thinking. He threw down the cards, slumped into the recliner and closed his eyes.

His head was spinning.

This is too much. I don't care, he thought. No, I *do* care. The Condors have to win. They just have to. But Ian was right...and so were Mom and Dad. This is crazy. It isn't fun anymore. It's become a nightmare, a nightmare that has to stop.

Donny opened his eyes. But the real nightmare had just begun.

On the coffee table, the starting line-up was neatly arranged. His posters were propped up on both sides of the TV. The pennants were in place, too, and his T-shirt was draped over the arm of the chair, with his cap balanced carefully on top of it. Everything was set up, ready for the game to start—but he hadn't done any of it.

His heart began to pound. He reached for his cap, ready to heave it across the room. But he couldn't. Instead, he felt his hand moving toward his head. Like a zombie following its master's orders, he put on his cap, flinching at its touch. This favorite of all his treasures had become a

thing of horror, something that made his skin crawl.

Terrified, Donny tried to fling himself out of the chair. I have to get out of here, he thought. But he couldn't move. An invisible force threatened to crush him each time he tried to push himself up.

Desperate, he opened his mouth to scream for help, but no sound emerged. Finally, he stopped struggling and collapsed limply in the chair. The game started. Through no choice of his own, he began to watch.

His last clear thought was that he hadn't made the popcorn. After that, everything blurred. He could see the TV set and hear the announcers' voices, but the picture and the words were hideously distorted.

Donny was terrified. He felt trapped in a kind of waking-dead zone where nothing made any sense...until two familiar words finally pierced the horrible blur.

Donny latched onto them like a drowning swimmer clutching a life preserver. He forced himself to focus on the familiar syllables. "Cracker Jacks." Then, an entire line echoed in his head—"I don't care if I never come back...don't care if I never come back...don't care...care...care."

But I *do* care, he screamed silently. I *want* to come back.

Suddenly, Donny realized that he could hear again—and see. On the TV screen, the crowd was on its feet, roaring out the words to "Take Me Out to the Ball Game."

Donny felt weak with relief. Without thinking, he reached up to scratch his head. As his hand touched the brim of his cap, the full impact of what he'd just done hit him. He'd moved on his own. Slowly, he lowered his arm and leaned forward. Then he carefully pushed himself out of the chair.

To reassure himself that the nightmare had truly ended, he ran a quick reality check. He focused on the screen, where a chart listed the runs, hits and errors for the first eight innings. He was able to read it and understand what it meant.

It showed that the Condors were behind by two runs. Too bad, he thought. He tensed, waiting for the frantic feeling that he had to do something to make his team win—but it didn't come.

He steadied himself against the coffee table and stepped away from the chair. Still nervous, he glanced back at the television. Farley, the Condors' star reliever, was winding up. The ball burned across the outside corner of the plate and Carter, the Falcon's slugger, was history.

Donny found himself hoping that the Condors would pull the game out of the fire when they got up to bat. Then he caught himself. It was bad luck to think of winning, wasn't it? No, it was bad luck only if you said your team was going to win when they were leading, not when they were behind. Besides, you had to say it out loud to jinx them. That's what Dad said, anyway. He said all baseball fans knew better than to jinx their team that way.

With this thought, Donny began to smile. One or two superstitions were okay. That was part of the fun of baseball.

He switched off the TV, picked up his pennant and headed upstairs, hoping he'd find Dad or Ian watching the game in the living room. He still wanted to see the bottom of the ninth, but it would be more fun if he could watch it with somebody.

The Empty Place

Mom pointed to the large hawk soaring above the cottage. "Look, Kit. Isn't it beautiful?"

Kit glanced skyward.

"So what?" she said sullenly. "It's just a bird." She turned her back and began to walk away.

"Kit? Where are you going?"

"Nowhere." Kit kept walking.

"Hold on, Kit. It's nearly lunch time. I want you to stay close to the cottage for now."

Kit took two more steps, then stopped as her little brother, Eugene, dashed out of the bushes beside the cottage. He came straight at her, arms outstretched.

"Hey, Kit, look what I found."

Carefully, he uncupped his hands. But not carefully enough. A bumpy brown toad leapt out just as Kit bent down to look.

"You brat," she hissed, jumping back.

"But, Kit, I never did it on purpose. Come on. Help me catch it again, will you?"

"You wish. Catch your own stupid toads—and keep them far away from me." Kit turned on her heel and stomped away.

"You're no fun anymore," Eugene yelled as he headed back behind the cottage, hot on the trail of the escaping amphibian.

His words pierced Kit with a guilt that nearly stopped her in her tracks. She knew she was acting like a jerk, but this knowledge just made her angrier—with herself and everybody else.

She hadn't asked to be included in the family's vacation at the cottage. In fact, she'd begged to stay behind in town, where she could watch TV, hang out with her friends and have some fun.

Kit kept walking. She wanted a space of her own, away from the rest of the family. She started to jog, then broke into a run.

"Kit, wait," she heard her mother call. Kit ignored her and kept running until she reached the cover of a nearby willow grove.

From her vantage point under the drooping branches, Kit watched her parents walk back to the picnic table and sit down. Eugene was already seated, getting a head start on the sandwiches.

"Guess who's missing from the happy holiday picture?" Kit muttered angrily. They're just fine, she thought. They can have lots of fun without me.

Turning away, she began to work her way through the willow branches. When she broke through to the other side of the grove, she took a deep breath and took off across the vast expanse of meadow that lay before her.

Kit ran and ran. She ran until her breathing was so harsh and shallow that she could run no more. She slowed to a jog, but finally had to stop. Gasping, she bent over, hands on her knees, and tried to catch her breath.

Gradually, the pounding in her chest lessened, and the pain in her side eased. She straightened up slowly and looked back the way she'd come. Far off, to the right, she could still see the dark outline of the woods ringing the lake, but she could barely pick out the cottage and the willow grove beside it.

Not far enough. I can still see it, Kit thought, and decided to keep going. "Until I don't have to see anyone or anything," she said aloud as she set off once more, this time at an easy jog.

She had no idea how long she'd been running when she started to pay attention to her surroundings again. The first thing she noticed was that the sun was no longer directly overhead. She could still feel its powerful rays on the back of her neck and shoulders, but it was definitely lower in the sky. Her lengthening shadow told her that.

Glancing down, she realized that the ground had changed, too. The soft meadow grasses were gone and, underfoot, dried weeds and withering wild strawberry plants crunched and crackled.

The sun's cooking you too, she mused, looking at the brown and red leaves clinging to a sandy patch of ground before her. Suddenly, a quick shadow streaked across her path. Kit turned and squinted over her shoulder into the sky.

Oh, it's you, she thought as she picked the large black hawk out of the sun's glare. Who invited you along? Go back to my mother. She's the bird lover, not me. Aloud she added, "This is my spot. Mine, you hear."

The realization that she had actually shouted these words left Kit feeling more than a little foolish.

Thank goodness no one is around to hear, she thought. But the words had struck a memory chord. Kit stopped walking and looked around again. Hey, maybe this really is my place, she thought, recalling the game she'd invented when she was little. She flopped onto the ground, thinking that she might finally be able to win it here.

Kit stretched out, her hands clasped under her neck, and began to move her eyes in every direction while keeping her head perfectly still.

"Nearly," she said, sitting up and yanking at a tall clump of chicory that had managed to survive the heat and sand. "Sorry, but you have to go," she announced. Then she lay back down and looked around again.

That's better, she thought. This place has definite possibilities. Then she saw the hawk again.

"Go away," she ordered. "This is my place. You're wrecking the game."

The hawk lingered briefly, suddenly swooped lower, then soared high and faded into the cloudless sky.

Finally, Kit thought. Nobody and nothing. I've finally found my empty place.

Her thoughts drifted back to the summer six years ago when she'd started her search for this place. That year, her family had spent their vacation at her uncle's farm. One day, lying on the roof of the cowshed with her cousins, Kit had found herself staring into an empty, clear blue sky. She had lain outside many times before—flat on her back on the apartment balcony, in the wading pool at the park, and even in the schoolyard. But this time was different.

This time, nothing, absolutely nothing had broken her view of the sky—no birds, no branches, no awnings, not even a hydro pole or telephone line. Suddenly, she'd been overwhelmed by the vast emptiness.

This is fun, she'd thought. It's like being all alone in the middle of nowhere, even though I'm really not. It felt good, being in the empty place she'd just discovered.

Keeping her head still, she'd let her eyes wander to the left. Still nothing. Once again, all she could see was blue. When she'd looked to the right, though, a tall tree had intruded into the blueness. Then two crows had risen squawking from the garden, flying directly into view, and the spell had been broken.

But the excitement of that moment had lingered. Several times that summer, she'd searched for a place where she could lie down, look up and around and see nothing but sky. It became a kind of game for her. She'd flop down, cushion her head with her hands, and try out a new place. But, no matter where she tried out the view, something—a tree or a bird or a single power line—always got in the way.

There was no point even trying on cloudy days. She would not allow the smallest wisp of white to drift by. That was against the rules, rules she'd come up with after that time on the cowshed roof. Only the sun was allowed. She couldn't look right at it anyway, so it didn't count. But anything else would break the spell cast by the emptiness.

When her cousins began to tease her about lying around all the time, just staring at the sky, she quickly learned to seek out her empty place only when she was alone. She came close sometimes, but she never did find it that summer.

When she returned to the city, thoughts of her summer quest faded. Once, in the winter, she had tried again at the park, after an unusually heavy snowfall. The sun was shining brightly and the park was blanketed in white. She lay down in the snow and looked all around but, try as she might, she could never eliminate the nearby highrises from the picture. No matter where she went in the park, she could still see at least one.

The next summer Kit gave up her search. She was lying with two of her friends on the teeter-totters in the park. The three of them were just lying there saying nothing, staring up at the sky.

When she asked them if they ever tried to find a place where they could see absolutely nothing but the sky, they looked at her as if she had grown antennae. "You're nuts, Kit," one of them had said. Embarrassed, Kit had vowed never to think about the stupid game again.

But here she was, two years later, absolutely spellbound because there was nothing, absolutely nothing, in sight. This is amazing, she thought. Nothing and nobody. Just what I wanted. I wonder how long it will last.

Now that she knew it was possible to find such a place, a new rule began to take shape in her mind. Once I find it, I can't move until something invades it, she thought.

"But that won't take long," she added aloud. "Something always comes along."

Kit lay still, staring upward at the seamless blue canopy, waiting for that something—a plane, a cloud, a bee buzzing by. She waited and waited, but nothing intruded into her empty place.

"Amazing," she repeated softly, relishing the moment.

Then her neck began to itch. Bet I've got a sunburn, she found herself thinking. Hope Mom brought the Noxzema. Don't be silly. Mom always remembers to bring the Noxzema. And the sun block...

Mom always remembers the air mattress, too. And a brand new jigsaw puzzle. Always a new puzzle. Wonder how many pieces this one will have? And the new game? What'll it be? *Balderdash*? I'll bet that's it. Have to wait to find out, though. It has to be a surprise...

Kit realized she was looking forward to finding out which games Mom had brought along. Okay, so maybe doing puzzles and playing games with the family isn't so bad, she thought. Maybe I won't be bored totally out of my mind.

Kit scanned the empty sky again. Her neck was getting stiff and she wanted to stand up and brush away the sand that was starting to make her skin itch. Okay, I've had enough. Time for something to break into the emptiness. Time to go home.

"Come out, come out, wherever you are," she called.

Maybe I goofed. Maybe I can see something, she thought, and forced her eyes from side to side as far as they could go. But she'd picked her spot well. Without turning her head, she couldn't see past the sandy patch where she had flopped down.

How long have I been here? she wondered. A long time. Shouldn't have pulled out that plant. Then I could have seen it—and I could have got up. Maybe I'll cheat. Turn my head a bit. I'm sure there was some tall grass just past the strawberry leaves. I remember that.

She checked the sky one last time. Empty. That's it, then. Time's up, she decided, and turned her head to the side. No tall grass there. She turned the other way. There was nothing there either.

"That's weird," Kit said softly. I was sure it was there, she thought. Oh well, I moved my head so the game's over anyway. I may as well get up.

Kit sat up and looked around. She rubbed her eyes and looked again. Impossible, she thought, and scrambled to her feet.

She stared in disbelief. For as far as she could see, there was absolutely nothing, nothing but the occasional wild strawberry runner clinging to the dry brown ground. It was as if the spot had spread out around her until it met the sky. The sweat trickling down her neck felt suddenly cold. It sent a shiver up her spine.

For a long time, Kit stood transfixed. Then she began to turn slowly, desperately scanning the horizon for anything that would help her get her bearings. She became frantic, looking—and looking again—for a familiar landmark. All she could see was acres of sand meeting the endless blue of the empty sky.

Feeling dizzy, she stopped turning and looked up again. The sun still shone, but it was much lower in the sky. Still, it couldn't help her. She had no idea whether the cottage lay north, south, east or west.

She wanted to run again. But she didn't know which way to go. For the second time that day, Kit began to cry. Sobbing, she felt very lost and alone.

She had no idea how much time had passed when she began to notice the breeze brushing against her tears. Gentle at first, it grew stronger with each gust. Thick white clouds edged with gray began to roll in, gobbling up the blue. Kit's heart raced. She could smell the approaching storm. Run, her mind screamed. Run. Run. Run.

Kit started to run, then turned and began to run in the opposite direction. "Which way? Which way?" she yelled into the terrible emptiness. Despairing, she stopped again, choking back her sobs.

It was then that she saw it. It was only a speck at first, a pinpoint of black in one of the last remaining patches of blue. When it disappeared behind a cloud, Kit thought she'd imagined it. But, seconds later, it was back, soaring and diving, its widespread wings riding the wind. Closer and closer it came, until it was directly overhead. It hovered for a moment, suspended in space. Then, with a mighty flap of its wings, it veered sharply back into the wind, struggling to return the way it had come.

Suddenly Kit realized where it had come from—and she knew where it was going. The voice inside her head became a chorus. Run. Run. Run. Kit began to run again, this time after the hawk.

They were going home.

Password to Mystery

I like my little sister, Jasmine. She's okay for a seven-year-old. So when I saw how upset she was that Mom didn't believe her, I felt I had to do something. For her sake—and for Mom's, too—I had to find out what really happened the day the garage burned down.

It wasn't that Mom—or anybody else—blamed Jasmine for the fire. The fire inspector said afterwards that a possum probably ate through the wiring and the old wooden building just went up like a tinderbox.

Besides, Jasmine wasn't anywhere near the garage when the fire started. And that's really what caused all the trouble—and plunked us into the middle of a mystery straight out of the *Twilight Zone.*

After school, Mrs. Bellamy, our next-door neighbor, babysits Jasmine until Mom gets home.

When Karen and David Bellamy, who go to a different school, get home, the three of them—Jasmine, Karen and David—go out and play.

Most days they play...well, used to play...in our garage. We don't have a car anymore, so Mom let us kids use it. There was a bench, three chairs, a table, an old radio and a bunch of other stuff in there.

On the day of the fire, the garage was already toast—burnt toast—by the time Mom got home from work. Fire trucks were everywhere.

The first thing Mom did was look for Jasmine, who was nowhere to be seen. And when Mrs. Bellamy said that she hadn't checked in after school, they both assumed the worst. Mom was a basket case and Mrs. Bellamy wasn't much better.

So when Jasmine came strolling up the street, licking the drips off an ice cream cone, they were both ecstatic. Mom gave Jasmine a huge hug, holding on to her as if she would never let go.

Once the fire trucks left and all the neighbors went home, though, things really started to get crazy. That's when Jasmine told Mom that she wasn't in the garage because she'd gone off with a stranger.

This little piece of news sent Mom right through the roof. And when Jasmine tried to calm her down by explaining that she only went with the woman because that's what Mom wanted, it just made things worse. In fact, Mom totally lost it.

She was sure Jasmine was making up the whole story to get out of explaining where she'd really been after school. She accused her of lying and sent her to bed right after dinner.

"When you're ready to tell the truth, young lady, you can come downstairs again," she said grimly.

What with Jasmine bawling in her room and Mom slamming dishes and pots around in the kitchen, the house was pretty tense. So I decided that it was time to step in and persuade Jasmine to come clean. And that's how I ended up sitting on the end of her bed listening to a really strange story.

"Vinnie," she said, snuffling into a soggy Kleenex, "the lady came up to me at the schoolyard gate and said Mom wanted me to go with her. She said, 'Unicorn,' so I knew it was okay."

"Unicorn" is our password. Mom picked it because she loves unicorns. She has lots of them. She used to collect them when she was young. She has two stuffed ones, a plastic one, a poster of one, a silver one, and her favorite—a tiny crystal one that sits on her dresser. Jasmine's always holding it up at the window so the sun can shine through it and make rainbows dance on the wall. But she's really careful because she knows how much Mom likes it.

Jasmine also said that the woman knew a lot about Mom.

"She knew lots of stuff, Vinnie. She knew Mom likes black cherry ice cream and cheeseburgers and red flowers."

"Did the lady say *how* she knew this stuff?"

"Nope," Jasmine answered miserably.

"Well, what did she say?"

Jasmine blew her nose again.

"Well, at the park, when we passed the roses, she asked if Mom still loved the red ones best."

"Wait a minute," I interrupted. "Are you sure she said *still* loved the red ones?"

Jasmine nodded.

"Now think hard, Jasmine. Try to remember exactly what she said when you first saw her."

"She was over by the gate and she said my name and I went over. Then she said, 'Your mom wants you to come with me.' So I asked her for the password—like I'm supposed to—and the lady just smiled...and then she said it. 'Unicorn.' So I went with her...to the park...and then to the ice cream store and..."

"Hold on, back up a minute. Did your friends see the lady at school?"

"I dunno. Maybe."

"Well, didn't you explain why you weren't walking home with them?"

"Nope, I already told them I was going to run home by myself."

"Why?"

" 'Cause I wanted to glue the sparkly stuff on the popsicle-stick box I made for Mrs. Bellamy. I left it on the table in the garage last night and I wanted to finish it and give it to her. It was supposed to be a surprise."

My stomach tightened. "Jasmine, do you understand what a close call this was? Do you know what would have happened if you'd gone to the garage like you planned?"

"I know, Vinnie, " she howled. "But I didn't—and I didn't burn up because I went with the lady."

Jasmine was pretty convincing. Besides, if she was going to make up a lie, why would she pick such a stupid one? One Mom and I would see right through the minute she opened her mouth?

I decided that I believed her. But I needed to find a way to convince Mom. If I could find out who the woman was, then Mom could check Jasmine's story with her—and the mystery would be solved. But I needed more information.

"Okay, Jasmine, who saw you with the lady? Maybe some other kids in the park? Or maybe the man at the ice cream store?"

Jasmine shrugged glumly. "I don't know. The lady gave me the money for the ice cream—a double scooper—and waited for me outside on that little white bench. You know the one I mean?"

I nodded, then had another thought.

"You mentioned cheeseburgers. Did you go for a cheeseburger? Did someone see you there?"

"Nope. I still had my ice cream. When we passed Best Fries, the lady asked me if I liked cheeseburgers, just like Mom. I said yes and she asked if I wanted one. But I still had my ice cream and, besides, I said I'd be too full to eat dinner. That's when she disappeared."

"Disappeared? You never said anything about disappearing before."

"Well, you never asked me."

"Okay, so I'm asking now. What happened?"

"Well, when I said the stuff about being too full to eat dinner, the lady looked at her watch. Then she said, 'I think you've been gone long enough,' and then I saw Vanessa and..."

"Hold on," I interrupted. "She said, 'You've been gone long enough'? You're sure that's what she said?"

"I'm sure."

I was confused. Why, I wondered, would the woman say something like that? Long enough for what? It didn't make any sense. Neither did the bit about her disappearing. Could Mom be right after all? Was Jasmine making it all up?

"All right. Go on. You saw Vanessa and then what?"

"Vanessa was across the street with her mom, so I waved and showed her my ice cream. And when I turned around again, the lady was gone. She was just...gone. So I came home...and the garage was on fire and Mom was crying and hugging me. And then later, she said I was lying and..."

Jasmine started bawling again. I waited until she calmed down a little, then tucked her in.

"Go to sleep now, you hear?" I said. She peeked out over the sheet and nodded.

As I got up to leave, I thought of one more question.

"Jasmine, what was the lady's name?"

Jasmine gave a little shrug.

"Didn't she tell you? Didn't she say 'Hi, I'm so-and-so' or something?"

"I forget," Jasmine whispered, rolling over to face the wall, "and I'm too tired to remember..."

The next morning, the house was still pretty miserable. Jasmine's eyes were swollen from all the crying she'd done and Mom was still pretty grim.

When I got home from school, I slipped up to Mom's bedroom and called some of Jasmine's friends to ask if they'd seen her with a stranger. The only clue I got was from Carla Muir.

"No, I didn't see Jasmine with anyone," she said. "The last time I saw her, she was standing at the schoolyard gate and then she just walked away by herself."

I went downstairs and found Jasmine at the kitchen table, her arithmetic workbook open in front of her. She was staring out the window, watching Karen and David Bellamy playing in the driveway.

"Want a popsicle?" I asked, opening the fridge.

"Nope."

"Suit yourself, but I've got a question. Remember yesterday when the lady met you at the gate?"

Jasmine nodded, but didn't look up.

"Well, how long did you wait before she came along?"

"She was there when I came out."

I was getting frustrated. "Look, Jasmine. Carla just told me she saw you at the gate—by yourself."

"I wasn't by myself," Jasmine said stonily. "The lady was there. I was talking to the lady."

Her face screwed up and I could tell the tears were about to flow again. I threw up my hands and went back upstairs. Jasmine's story wasn't hanging together. I decided to make one last phone call. After that, I didn't know what I was going to do.

Vanessa's mother, Mrs. Hall, answered on the fourth ring. "Mrs. Hall, do remember seeing my sister yesterday afternoon, outside Best Fries?"

"Oh, yes. Vanessa and I were on the way to the library. Her books were overdue."

Finally, I thought. Now I could get some answers about the mysterious stranger.

"Did you happen to notice who she was with, Mrs. Hall?"

"Who she was with? She wasn't with anyone, Vinnie. She was just standing there, by herself, eating an ice cream cone."

"She wasn't with a woman?"

"No...but, wait, let me think...maybe there was someone inside the restaurant. Jasmine did seem to be talking to someone, though I couldn't see who it was. She was waving her ice cream cone around and smiling."

"That's great, Mrs. Hall. Can you remember anything else?"

"Not really. Jasmine just waved to us, then stood there looking around. Then she walked away. Why are you asking all these questions?"

"Oh, it's nothing, Mrs. Hall."

I thanked her and got off the phone. But I wondered why I'd said thank you. What I'd just

heard left me more uncertain than ever. If Jasmine had gone off with someone, she was the only one who had seen her. Either that, or Jasmine had started talking to herself in a big way. Somehow, the mess I'd set out to clear up was becoming more muddled than ever.

Later that night, after Jasmine was in bed, I told Mom what I'd found out. She was puzzled, too. We went round and round in maybe circles—maybe Jasmine did this, maybe she did that, maybe she, maybe, maybe, maybe. Nothing made sense. Finally, Mom came up with one more maybe.

"Vinnie, maybe Jasmine just imagined the lady, like little kids sometimes imagine a playmate. I did when I was little. And so did Dawn. You remember me telling you about Dawn?"

Mom paused for a moment, lost in thought. She hadn't mentioned her best friend, Dawn, in years. Not since she'd gotten the news that Dawn and her two little boys had died in a fire. Jasmine had been a baby at the time and Dad had still been around, too.

I remember the day the letter arrived. I came home from school and Dad was there, holding Jasmine. Mom was sitting on the couch holding the letter and wiping tears from her eyes.

Mom walked over to the buffet and took her old photograph album from the bottom drawer. She came back to the couch and began turning the pages slowly. Finally, she stopped at a picture of two young girls grinning at the camera, each clutching a stuffed unicorn.

"That's me and that's Dawn. We were ten then. It was amazing, Vinnie. We both loved the same things, even unicorns. Can you believe it? She gave me that little crystal one on my dresser just before she moved to Guatemala."

She flipped to a picture of two young women wearing gowns and mortar boards. They were smiling for the camera and clutching diplomas.

"She was such a special friend, Vinnie. We were always there for each other until..."

She stopped when she heard the footsteps on the stairs. Jasmine appeared, rubbing the sleep from her eyes.

"What are you doing up, honey?" Mom asked, motioning for Jasmine to join us on the couch. "Did you have a bad dream?"

Jasmine nodded and snuggled between us. Mom put the photo album on the coffee table and turned to give her a cuddle. But Jasmine suddenly squirmed away.

"You found her, you found her!" she whooped.

"Found who?" Mom asked.

"The lady! There." Jasmine was pointing at the graduation picture of Mom and Dawn. "You found her, didn't you, Vinnie? I knew you would." She threw her arms around my neck.

Stunned, I looked over her head at Mom. Mom stared back at me, then looked back at the picture. Finally, she broke the silence.

"Jasmine, come here," she said, patting her lap. Jasmine shifted over. "Now, look at me. Are you saying this is the lady you went with after school?"

"Yes, yes, yes!" Jasmine bubbled.

This time, it was Mom who looked over Jasmine's head at me. She looked confused, maybe even a little frightened. I know that's how I felt. I felt goose bumps on my neck. Had Dawn really come back from the grave to save my little sister?

Jasmine looked up at Mom.

"Mom? She's your friend, isn't she? You just forgot about her, didn't you?"

"You're right, Jasmine," she said softly. "I just forgot about her. She was a very special friend. Now, it's way past your bedtime. But I promise, I'll tell you all about her one day."

The Newcomer

Raffi knew exactly how it felt to be the new kid. He remembered his own first day at Langley—and how nervous he'd been.

So when he spotted Damien, all alone, leaning against the schoolyard fence, he walked over.

"Hi," he said, trying to sound friendly, but not pushy. "I'm Raffi Kadir."

"Hi, I'm Raffi Kadir," Damien repeated snarkily.

Startled, Raffi blurted, "What's the matter with you?"

"What's the matter with you?" Damien parroted.

"Hey, come on. I was just trying to..."

Before Raffi finished, Damien was already repeating his words, like an evil echo. Turning away, Raffi muttered, "Forget it."

He flinched as Damien spat back, "Forget it."

"So...what's he like?" Tommy Lo Presti asked as Raffi rejoined the cluster of kids gathered near the door. Tommy glanced warily at Damien before continuing. "Did you ask where he came from?"

"Nope," Raffi shrugged.

When Mrs. Mullen had introduced Damien to the class and asked him to say something about himself, he'd simply shaken his head. At the time, Raffi had thought that the newcomer was just shy. Now he wasn't so sure.

"Maria says he just stared at her when she tried to talk to him," Jenny Clayton added in a low voice. "Remember when she was handing out the magnifying glasses? She says he's scary."

"So?" Raffi said, trying to sound calmer than he felt. "People say lots of things about a new kid, right?"

"Yeah, but..." Tommy argued, "this guy could be trouble. I mean, look at what he's doing right now." He added quickly, "But don't stare."

Damien had grabbed a soccer ball from a group of third-graders. He was holding it at arm's length, out of their reach. One boy jumped up and grabbed Damien's arm, trying to drag it and the ball down. Damien shook him off like a fly. Then he drew back his arm and heaved the ball all the way to the far end of the yard.

At that moment, the bell rang and everyone, including Damien, started toward the door.

By lunch time, Raffi had nearly forgotten the nastiness at recess. So it took him a while to catch on to what was happening behind his back as he walked to the cafeteria.

First, he noticed two little kids outside Miss Daneff's room staring past him. Then he heard the giggling. He turned quickly, and caught Damien turning too, just a few steps behind him. Three eighth-grade girls farther back snickered.

A feeling of helplessness washed over Raffi. He knew exactly what would happen the instant he turned around again. Damien would follow him, imitating everything he did.

"What's with you?" Raffi asked.

"What's with you?" Damien repeated, without turning to face Raffi.

Quickly, Raffi moved toward Damien and stepped in front of him. "I was just trying to be friendly. Guess I was stupid, eh?"

Without waiting, he strode deliberately past his tormentor to the cafeteria. As he pushed open the door, he enjoyed a brief moment of satisfaction. Damien had made it all the way to "stupid" before he caught on.

But Raffi's victory was fleeting. During lunch, Damien positioned himself at the next table and mirrored his every move.

He even managed to win over a small audience of nervous fifth-graders desperate to avoid becoming victims themselves.

During afternoon classes, Damien toned down the attack somewhat. But even though the teacher noticed nothing unusual, Raffi knew what was going on behind his back. And he felt powerless to combat it.

The next two days were Raffi's worst ever at Langley. His only defense was to keep away from the tall, glowering newcomer whenever he could and to say as little as possible. He even stopped putting up his hand to answer questions for fear of hearing the vicious whisper parroting his words from two seats back and one over.

When his friends asked him what he was going to do, he shrugged and told them he could handle it. Sounding more confident than he felt, he said that Damien would soon get bored with his stupid game and everything would be fine again.

"Maybe you should tell Mrs. Mullen," Jenny suggested.

Tommy rolled his eyes, saying this would probably only make matters worse.

But Jenny persisted. "Mrs. Mullen says she won't stand for bullying, and this is bullying, that's for sure. I bet she can help."

"Maybe," Raffi agreed, "but Tommy's probably right. Anyway, what am I going to say? That Damien is driving me crazy by acting like my shadow? I'll sound like an idiot."

"She'd understand."

"Maybe, but *he* wouldn't," Tommy shot back. "What do you say we get some of the guys together and make him understand?"

The thought of beating up someone horrified Raffi, but he didn't say so. Instead he simply repeated that he could take whatever Damien was dishing out.

"Well, I couldn't," Jenny admitted. "I still think you should tell Mrs. Mullen. She'd understand. Or how about your mom or dad. They would too, I bet."

By Friday, however, Raffi doubted whether Mrs. Mullen or his parents would understand what was happening between him and Damien. He didn't think anyone would. Why should they, he thought. It was impossible.

Impossible as it seemed, though, Raffi was convinced that Damien was no longer just one nerve-racking step behind him. He was now a sinister sidekick, lifting a hand exactly when Raffi did, reaching for a sandwich or opening his locker at exactly the same moment, even saying or whispering the few words that Raffi still spoke in exactly the same breath. There was no longer a time delay on the bully's broadcast network.

After school on Friday, Raffi hid in the washroom until he figured the coast was clear. Then, he slipped out of the building and, like a lone rider waiting to be ambushed, cautiously worked his way home.

The dreaded Damien never materialized. Raffi made it safely to his house but, even after slamming the door behind him, he didn't feel safe. Shaded windows and thick brick walls were useless barriers against someone who seemed to be able to tune in his thoughts at will. Raffi tossed his bag behind the coat rack and threw himself on the couch, face down.

That's where his dad found him a few minutes later.

"I thought I heard you come in," Mr. Kadir said. "Here, look at this one."

Raffi glanced at the watch his dad was holding out. The back was open and he could see the tiny brass wheels and gears turning smoothly.

"Isn't it a beauty?" Mr. Kadir continued. "Lucy Vanier brought it in yesterday. It was her great-great-grandfather's. I couldn't resist working on it right away. Just one little spring—that's all it needed. And now it's ticking away like new again."

"Just a spring, eh?" Raffi asked, trying to sound interested in the work that brought his dad such satisfaction.

"That's all. She wound it too tight by mistake, and it just snapped."

I know how that feels, Raffi thought, watching his dad's long, thick fingers gently close the watch. It never ceased to amaze him that a man with such big hands could do such delicate work.

Mr. Kadir palmed the watch in his left hand and reached out with the other to brush the hair off Raffi's forehead. He frowned and asked, "Everything okay, son?"

Raffi rolled over, hoping his eyes wouldn't betray the turmoil he felt.

"I'm fine, Dad. Leave me alone, okay? I'm just tired"

"And a bit touchy too, eh? Your mom won't be home from work for another hour. Why don't you grab a nap? I'll be down in the shop if you need me."

"Sounds good," Raffi mumbled, turning his face back into the cushion.

"I'm beat," he added, shutting his eyes. Within a few minutes he was lost in sleep, but it was a sleep that brought him no rest.

The dream was painfully real. He was running—from a monstrous, twisted version of Damien that was reaching toward him with long, talon-like fingers. "You can't get away, Raffi," it intoned as it drew ever closer. "There's plenty of room in here for me," it said as the hands began to claw at Raffi's hair. "I'm coming in."

Raffi woke with a start. He was sweating and gasping for breath, as if he had actually been running. He sat up and leaned against the back of the couch, trying to calm down. Some of the nightmare's details were already fading, but not the fear it had created—and not Damien's words.

"You can't come in," Raffi whispered to the empty room. But, he wondered as he pushed himself up, how do I keep him out? Feeling helpless, Raffi dragged himself into the kitchen, toward the comforting sound of his parents' voices and dishes rattling. He couldn't stand another minute alone.

Miserable as he was, Raffi told his parents nothing, not even when his mother asked straight out if something was bothering him. Instead, he mumbled that he felt crummy and said he'd decided to go to bed early.

He didn't like lying, but he knew exactly how they'd react if he told them the truth. They'd be worried and angry and they'd probably want to call

the principal. As he headed upstairs, he thought, That's all I need. My parents talking to the principal. Then the whole school will think I'm a wimp.

As he slipped under the covers, he decided he'd just have to wait until Damien stopped.

But, as he surrendered to an overwhelming fatigue, Raffi was haunted by the thought that Damien would never stop. Damien would go on and on, until he got what he wanted—whatever that was. Then he'd find another victim and the vicious game would start all over again.

Raffi managed to survive the rest of the weekend without arousing his parents' suspicions that anything really serious might be wrong. When Tommy dropped by Saturday afternoon to see if he wanted to shoot some baskets, he said he was still feeling too crummy.

And he dredged up the too-much-homework routine to avoid joining the kids on a visit to the new virtual reality exhibit at the Science Center. This was hard to pass up, but keeping out of Damien's line of fire was the only defense he felt he had. Besides, he wasn't sure he could stomach any more virtual reality than he was already experiencing. Damien couldn't be real. Real people couldn't do what he did.

Monday morning brought with it the harsh realization that hiding out was no longer an option. Filled with dread, Raffi dressed slowly, dragging on a clean pair of jeans, an old green T-shirt and his well-worn Giants cap. Halfway through his Shreddies, the knot building in his stomach tightened and he put down his spoon, unable to take another bite.

After pouring the leftover cereal down the sink when Dad wasn't looking, he moved to the hall, picked up his bag and opened the door. As it closed behind him, he called out a quick good-bye. He had to get away before his parents saw the look he was sure must be in his eyes, the haunted look of someone trapped in a hopeless situation. Shoulders sagging, he set out for school.

It wasn't until he wandered into his home room two minutes after the bell rang that he realized the full extent of Damien's power. As he passed the seat two behind and one over from his, a flash of green caught his eye. There was Damien, smirking. He was wearing blue jeans, a green T-shirt and a well-worn Giants cap.

Before Raffi could gasp, Damien beat him to it. Then he said, "We're wearing the same clothes."

Raffi was horrified. The same words had just flashed through his own mind. It had finally happened. His nightmare had come true. Damien was in his head, thinking his thoughts, making the same choices he did.

Like a deer frozen in a spotlight, Raffi stood in the aisle, his breath coming in short gasps. His eyes blurred and tears began to scald his cheeks. Humiliated, he turned and ran from the classroom, ignoring Mrs. Mullen's plea to stop.

His mother had left for work when Raffi arrived back home, but the squeaky floorboards in the hall gave him away. From his repair shop in the basement, his father called out loudly, "Who's there?"

"Just me, Dad," Raffi called back, trying to stop his voice from cracking. "Feeling sick again. Going to bed. That's all."

Raffi made it all the way to his room and into bed before he heard the phone. It rang just once. Good, he thought, figuring a customer's call would distract his father. But, moments later, Dad was standing in the doorway.

"Raffi, that was Mrs. Mullen. What happened?"

Fighting for control, Raffi outlined his torment. He told Dad about Damien and the laughter of the other kids. He didn't—he couldn't—tell him about how Damien had finally invaded his mind. Instead, afraid to say more, he clenched his fist and began punching his pillow.

"Bet you wish that pillow was him," Dad said softly, sitting on the bed beside him.

Raffi nodded weakly.

"Bullies can do that to you—make you want to punch their faces in. But that's not you, is it?"

Raffi nodded again and gave the pillow a last feeble punch.

"Or they can make you run and hide. Either way, they've got you, right? The turf is theirs. They just take over."

Mr. Kadir placed his hand on Raffi's shoulder. "Look at me, son."

Raffi looked up at his dad.

"Do you want me to go back to school with you?" Raffi shook his head.

"Okay. Then how about talking to Mrs. Mullen? She's worried about you and I know she could help."

Again, Raffi shook his head.

"All right. Maybe what you need right now is time, time to think this through. But promise me one thing. Promise me you'll ask for help if you need it. That's the other way a bully gets you, by making you afraid to do that. Promise?"

Raffi promised and, after letting his dad tuck the covers around him, lay alone and exhausted, staring blankly at the ceiling. In his mind, he replayed the horrors of the last week. Like a videotape running in reverse, he started with Damien's ghoulish triumph an hour earlier and worked backwards through the less deadly days of shadow dancing to the petty parroting that had started it all off last Monday.

At this point, Raffi hit his mental pause button. He managed a small smile when he recalled how he had nearly trapped Damien into saying, "Guess I was stupid."

Damien had seemed human enough that day, with his evil powers still under wraps. Maybe, Raffi wondered, I could have stopped him back then, done something, told somebody. But it was too late now. Damien's powers had been revealed and, as if feeding on something, they were growing stronger.

Raffi froze this frame for a moment. He approached it carefully, poking at it to see if it would snarl and poke back. It didn't. It lay still in his head, waiting for him to make sense of it. When he did, a glimmer of hope and the vague outline of a plan emerged from his frustration and desperation.

Raffi pushed himself up and sat on the edge of the bed, letting his plan take shape. When he had filled in a few missing details, he still wasn't sure it would work. But he was sure of one thing—he had to give it a try.

He considered changing his clothes, but quickly dismissed this idea. "I can wear what I want," he said aloud as he stood up.

He jammed his feet into his sneakers, grabbed his cap from the bed and headed downstairs. He walked over to the bench where his dad was working on an old mantel clock.

"Feeling better, son?" Mr. Kadir began, but Raffi interrupted.

"Dad, I know this is going to sound really weird, but I've got to ask you something. Would you call Mrs. Mullen for me?"

"No problem. I'm sure she'll have a talk with this kid and..."

"No, Dad. No. That's not what I want. Please, could you just call her and tell her I'm on my way back to school—and ask her not to say a word when I walk in?"

"Of course," Dad said guardedly. "But you're not going to do anything foolish?"

Knowing what Dad was afraid of, Raffi reassured him with a grin, saying quickly, "Don't worry, Dad. That's not me, remember?"

As he bounded up the stairs and out of the house, he added, "You can tell her if I need her help I'll ask for it, okay?"

"You will?"

"I will, Dad, for sure."

The fear Damien created was still with him when Raffi reached the school, but he was no longer fighting it. Instead, he was counting on it to act as a distraction. If his plan worked, Damien would be so busy feeding on that fear that he wouldn't realize what was happening.

He paused at the school door, took a deep breath and walked in. He passed the office and headed down the long hall to his home room. As he got closer, he saw that the door was open.

When he slipped into the back of the classroom, Mrs. Mullen stared at him for a moment, as if to make sure of something. Then she looked back at the class without saying a word.

Raffi stood perfectly still and focused on the desk two back and one over from his own. He gauged the distance between himself and his desk, and between Damien and Mrs. Mullen. Then he concentrated fiercely. Nothing happened.

Frantic, Raffi tightened every muscle in his body and concentrated even harder.

At last, Damien started to move. Slowly, he stood up and took a step forward. Raffi did the same. The rest of the class—and Mrs. Mullen—watched in silence.

Step after step, Raffi followed—until Damien stopped in front of Mrs. Mullen. Raffi stopped, too, right beside his own desk. Then he focused on each word of the silent speech he'd prepared.

Damien's words sounded wooden, almost mechanical, but they were loud and clear.

"Damien is a bully, but he's not going to win. Raffi is fighting back. Damien is a bully, but he's not going to..."

The snickers came first, followed by giggles. Then Tommy blurted out, "Right on!" and the clapping started.

His face twisted with rage, Damien swung around to face the class. His mouth moved, but no words came out. He lurched forward and headed down the aisle. Raffi stepped aside to let him pass. The slamming of the door echoed off the walls, then the room went quiet.

Like a spring that's wound too tight, then released, Raffi suddenly felt weak. His legs went slack and he slumped into his seat, blushing slightly. How, he thought, am I ever going to explain this?

As if reading his mind, Mrs. Mullen called the class to order, adding, "Let's give Raffi some time to unwind. We'll talk about this later."

Raffi grinned his thanks. He had no idea what he was going to say when everyone started asking questions, but at least he'd have time to think about it. And since he was thinking for himself again, he figured he might come up with some pretty good answers.

Something in the Air

Carly loved to feel her long hair drifting softly over her back—and she especially loved the strangely muted underwater rumblings echoing around her. She pressed her lips tighter and puffed out her cheeks, determined to hold her breath just a little longer. Then, with a final kick she broke the surface, gasping for air. That's when she saw it, bobbing just out of reach.

At first she wasn't sure what it was. Carly pushed her hair back from her face and wiped the water from her eyes. Whatever it was, it was red, glinting like a ruby in the sun.

Carly reached toward it, but a sudden wave pushed her forward and drove it under the water. She steadied herself in the sand underfoot. There it was again, bobbing in the surf. Carly lunged forward and grabbed it, going under as she did so.

When she surfaced, she found herself holding a red glass bottle not much bigger than her hand.

In the top was a weathered cork stopper. Excited, Carly held the bottle up to the light, looking for the rolled-up message she was sure she'd see inside. To her surprise, she saw nothing except a dull, smoky smudge near the bottom.

Rats, she thought. She'd already imagined herself on TV, reading a message from somebody up in Nova Scotia or down in Mexico. But there was no note, no secret message, no plea for help from a sailor stranded on a desert island.

Still, Carly was curious. This wasn't just any old bottle. Narrow at the neck, it flared out like a small wine glass sitting on a dainty little stand. It was a little like a fancy perfume bottle. Maybe that's what it is, she thought, and began to tug at the stopper. It was stuck.

She grasped the neck of the bottle firmly in her left hand and the stopper in her right. Carefully, she twisted the cork back and forth. Finally, with a small pop, it was out.

Carly peered into the bottle to make sure it really was empty. It was. She couldn't even see the smoky smudge anymore. Disappointed, she jammed the cork back in place. Time, she decided, to dry off and warm up a little.

She headed for shore, bouncing on her tiptoes as the waves carried her in. The breeze seemed to have died and a strange smell hung in the air. Old was the only word she could think of to describe it. It carried with it unusually strong hints of fish, salt and kelp. It was as if the bottom of the sea had bubbled up, releasing smells that had accumulated over hundreds of years.

By the time Carly reached the beach, the breeze had picked up and the smell wasn't so strong. Toweling off, she joined her friend, Maria, on their blanket.

Maria pushed herself up on one elbow, wrinkled her nose and said, "Do you smell that? What is it?"

"Yeah, I noticed it, too," Carly said. "It was stronger out there," she said, nodding toward the water. "But, here, look what I found." She held out the bottle.

Maria took it and held it up to the light.

"Neat. Where did you find it?"

Carly told her as she pulled on her T-shirt and shorts, then sniffed the air cautiously.

"Why don't we head home?" she asked. "That smell is bugging me. Besides, the sun block is worn off and I don't feel like gooping it on again."

Maria agreed, and the two girls packed up their things and headed for the boardwalk.

"I love the beach, don't you?" Carly said. "I wish we didn't have to go to school tomorrow. It's supposed to be ninety again. Can you believe it?"

"Yes, I can, and school's going to be awful. But there's only one week left. Just think. Only five more days till the summer holidays. We'll be free."

Carly followed as Maria ran ahead, shouting, "Free, free, free." When they reached Sandy Cove Road, the two friends parted, agreeing to meet before school the next morning. But that meeting was not meant to be.

Monday morning, Carly woke up barely able to swallow. She had a raging sore throat and her head was throbbing. After struggling to the bathroom, she crawled back into bed.

"Mom," she moaned when she heard her mother's footsteps. "Mom, I'm sick."

"Phew, what's that smell?" Mrs. Mackay asked as she walked into Carly's room. "Did you forget to unpack your beach bag again?"

"Guilty," Carly groaned, "but, Mom, have I got a fever? My throat's killing me and my head is exploding."

Mrs. Mackay picked her way through the litter on the floor and placed her hand on Carly's forehead.

"You do feel warm," she said. "And your eyes look shiny too. Open up. Say ahhh."

After peering into Carly's mouth, Mrs. Mackay announced that she'd have to stay home from school. "I'll be back in a minute with some juice and Tylenol, and then we'll check this mess and see if we can find what's smelling up this room."

"Mom," Carly mumbled, "could you call Maria and tell her I can't meet her?"

"Sure," Mrs. Mackay said, pushing Carly's hair off her forehead. "And I'll get the fan while I'm at it. Today is supposed to be another scorcher."

A few minutes later, Mrs. Mackay was back with the juice, pills and fan.

"Wouldn't you know it," she said, holding out a glass. "Maria is sick too."

"What's wrong with her?" Carly asked as she struggled to sit up.

"Same symptoms. There must be a bug going around." Mrs. Mackay dumped Carly's knapsack onto the mat. "Now let's get this gear into the wash."

"What's this?" she asked, holding up the red bottle.

"Oh, that," Carly muttered. "It's just an old bottle. I found it at the beach."

"It's pretty. I'll put it over here on your dresser."

"Sure, Mom, okay," Carly closed her eyes, and let her voice drift to a whisper.

She woke in a daze, blinking to adjust to the mid-afternoon sun flooding in through the window. The pain in her head was nearly gone. She sat up and looked around. Her room was spotless.

Mom must have tidied up while she slept. Carly took a few sips of juice and decided she might live. Her throat wasn't as sore as it had been, and she no longer felt as if she were burning up.

Still, something wasn't quite right. Finally, it hit her. The smell. It was still there, lingering like an invisible presence.

Carly threw off the sheet and headed downstairs. She found her mother in the backyard weeding the tomatoes.

"So, you finally surfaced. How do you feel?"

"Better, I think. Just a little woozy."

Mrs. Mackay brushed off her hands and felt Carly's forehead.

"The fever's gone. But, wait a minute...," she grimaced. She sniffed Carly's hair.

"Did you have a shower last night? Your hair smells...well...peculiar, just like your beach things did."

"Oh great," Carly answered, trying to sound upbeat. "My mother thinks I stink. Yes, I had a shower last night. Are you sure it's me? It's probably just something in the air. Maria and I noticed it yesterday."

"This is something only a mother can say, but...it's you, daughter dearest. Now, if you feel up to it, you should take care of that hair."

Carly trudged slowly up to the bathroom. She shampooed her hair twice. But when she reached out to grab her towel, she noticed that the scent of the apple shampoo wasn't the only smell in the steamy air. It also held the acrid smell of the sea.

It's here, too, Carly thought. Quickly, she wrapped herself in the towel and stepped onto the bath mat. Then she grabbed another towel from the shelf, twisted it around her head like a turban, and scurried down the hall to her room.

Through her window, a breeze was blowing. The smell was very faint, but it was still there. All she wanted to do was get away from it.

She got dressed and combed her hair, then scooped up the damp towels and quickly left the room. She tossed the towels into the laundry basket on the landing, muttering, "Out, out, horrid smell." Then she headed downstairs and dialed Maria's number.

"How are you feeling?" she asked when Maria came to the phone.

"Not too bad now, but I thought I was going to die this morning."

"Me too."

"Yeah, well, next time keep your wishes to yourself, okay?"

"What do you mean?"

"Yesterday, remember?" Maria said. "You said you wished we didn't have to go to school today, right? Well, your wish came true, didn't it?"

"Yeah, but...," Carly began.

"So next time," Maria teased, "wish for a million dollars or Johnny Depp or something, okay?"

"I'll see what I can do," Carly teased back. "Tomorrow morning, then? Usual time?"

"Yup," Maria groaned.

Then, trying to sound casual, Carly asked, "I was wondering. Did your clothes smell funny when you got home?"

"No. Why?"

"No reason. Forget it. See ya." Carly hung up before Maria could ask any more questions.

She found her mom sitting on the couch in the back room and leaned over, letting her damp curls fall in front of her mother's face.

"Do I pass the sniff test?"

Smiling, Mrs. Mackay assured her that her hair smelled fine. "You're probably right about that smell being something in the air. I noticed it again just as you came in, when the breeze came up. See," she pointed to the moving curtains, "if that keeps up, we might even get some sleep tonight."

But sleep was a long time coming for Carly that night, and not because of the heat. She could feel the cooling breeze blowing gently off the ocean, but neither the breeze nor the fan, turned to HIGH, could rid her room of the strange smell.

And, try as she might, Carly couldn't rid her mind of the thought that had crept in during dinner when Dad had frowned and asked about the strange smell. When her mom said that it was just something in the air, it had occurred to Carly that the mysterious something was linked to her.

Carly lay stiffly under the sheet, worrying about what was going to happen at school the next day. What am I going to do if the smell is still around? she wondered.

The annoying beep-beep of the digital clock revived her the next morning. She shut off the alarm and sat up. Swallowing hard, she turned her head from side to side to make sure yesterday's symptoms were gone. She felt fine. Then, nervously, she breathed in deeply through her nose. The smell was still there. Suddenly, she dreaded going to school.

She dressed slowly, but moved quickly when she left her room. In and out of the bathroom, in and out of the kitchen, right back upstairs. She made sure she wasn't in the same room with her mom and dad for more than a few seconds. Back in her room, she slowed down again.

What am I going to do at school? she asked herself as she braided her hair. The worried face in the mirror had no answer. As she reached for a hair clip, she noticed the red bottle, glowing in the morning sun.

It gave her an idea. She tiptoed into her parents' room and grabbed one of the small bottles on her mother's dresser.

Yuck, she thought when she took off the lid. Why do people wear this stuff, anyway? But she felt she had no choice. She grimaced as she dabbed perfume on her wrists, neck and shoulders. Then she headed back to her room.

Glancing in the mirror, she noticed the red bottle reflected in the glass. Suddenly, it struck her. The trouble with the smell had started right after she found the bottle. She reached for it, pulled out the cork, and sniffed cautiously. The whiff of sea smells tinged with something sweet and smoky made her flinch.

Carly jammed the cork back in place. So there was something smelly in the bottle—and I let it out, she thought. But smells don't hang around forever. It'll go away...I hope. She grabbed her knapsack and left her room, closing the door behind her.

Maria was waiting at the corner. "Carly, are you sure you're better? You look kinda pale." Suddenly, she wrinkled her nose. "And what's that gross smell?"

Carly's heart sank. She couldn't stand it anymore. The question made her want to scream. But Maria was still talking.

"Perfume," Maria squealed. "You're wearing perfume. And it stinks. You can't go to school smelling like this. Are you out of your mind?"

Carly burst into tears. As Maria tried to comfort her, she blurted out what had been happening.

"...so I put on some perfume. But it just made things worse. I really wish I hadn't put it on."

"Carly, that's too weird. I...," Maria stopped. A strange look came over her face as she took a step toward Carly and sniffed.

"Carly, I can't smell the perfume anymore." Suddenly, she grimaced. "But I can sure smell something else. Oh Carly, it's the beach smell."

Maria jumped back, fanning the air with her hand, as if to drive away the smell. Then, her eyes widened.

"Just a minute," she began slowly. "I know this sounds stupid, but think about it, Carly. On Sunday, you wished we didn't have to go to school. And your wish worked."

"Worked?" Carly laughed. "Maria, I got sick and so did you!"

"Well, maybe it didn't work quite the way you wanted, but it did work. And just now, you wished you hadn't put on that gross perfume. And I can't smell it anymore. Can you?"

"No, but…"

Excitedly, Maria clutched Carly's arm. "Remember Aladdin? What if there really was something in that bottle after all? Something smelly and invisible, just waiting to get out? And what if it gave you three wishes? You've used up two, but maybe you've still got one left."

Maria threw her arms wide and danced up and down. "Carly," she bubbled, "we could be rich! We could be famous! We could be…"

"…late for school, Maria," Carly managed to squeeze in, but Maria didn't seem to hear.

"Carly, we could have anything we want. But we have to be really careful. We have to think about it. We can't waste the last wish. What would you wish for?"

"You already know my wish, Maria. I wish this smell would go away."

"Carleeeee. Nooooo," Maria wailed.

Carly stared at her friend in stunned silence. "You weren't serious, were you?" she mumbled.

Maria hesitated, then sighed and shrugged. "No, of course not. I mean, really, what a dorky idea." She stopped and sniffed, "Anyway, I can't smell a thing. Your mom was probably right. It was just something in the air."

As they turned toward the school, Carly noticed that a breeze had sprung up. It felt cool against her cheek and smelled fresh and summery, the way it should on a day like this.

"Yeah," she said softly. "It was just something in the air."

Night Games

L uke had never stayed home alone at night. And convincing his mom that he was old enough to look after himself for a few hours took some doing.

"I don't like to leave you by yourself way out here. I wish Stephanie were here," she sighed.

"Well, Stephanie's at college now, Mom. She's two hundred miles away, so she can't just zip home and stay with me. Besides, I'd rather stay alone. Stephanie used to scare me to death. The minute you guys walked out the door, she'd start in about the hideous, slime-covered monsters in the basement."

"She didn't!"

"She did. And that's not all. She'd drag up every scary story she could think of and tell me all the gory details. I'm better off alone. Right, Dad?" Luke appealed to his father.

"Well, we won't be that far away, so I suppose..."

Luke grabbed the opening. "See, Mom. Dad thinks I'll be fine, too."

Luke eventually succeeded in wearing her down. But when it was time to go, it took her five minutes to run through a list of what-to-do-ifs....

Then she started on the next list. "Now remember, the nachos are in the cupboard over the stove and...."

"Mom, I live here, remember."

"All right," she laughed. "Now, you're sure you remember where I wrote the phone number where you can reach us?"

"Yes, Mom. It's stuck to the fridge door, Mom."

"And, one last thing. No one comes over, right?"

"Are you kidding, Mom? The action starts as soon as you leave. I told everybody to come over for a plate-breaking party. Which should we start with—the good dishes or the everyday ones?"

"I suppose you think that's funny?" Mom asked, trying to keep a straight face.

"Dad, take her away, please."

His dad obliged and Luke locked the door behind them. Then he let out a whoop, dashed into the living room and dove onto the couch. With no one around to complain, he channel-surfed for nearly an hour.

When he couldn't find anything he wanted to watch at 8:30, he headed for the kitchen. Popcorn, chips or nachos, or maybe even all of them? he asked himself. This is great, he gloated, trying to make up his mind.

He settled on nachos, but not just any old nachos straight from the bag. He opened the fridge and got out the cheese, a tomato, two green onions and the salsa. Then he scoured the shelves until he came up with a tin of colossal-sized black olives.

These are going to be amazing, he drooled, as he chopped, sliced and grated. When the plate was heaped to overflowing, he popped it into the microwave, set the timer to four minutes, and stood back to watch.

He was back in front of the television by 8:59, nachos on his lap. As the opening credits for *Young Samurai* started to roll, he felt on top of the world. This staying alone is a piece of cake, he thought. But seconds later, he was on his feet.

The noise—a scratching, tapping sound—had come from the basement. Luke moved quietly into the hall and stood at the top of the stairs, listening. There it is again, he thought.

His stomach tightened. Visions of Stephanie's slimy monsters sprang into his head.

Maybe I should call the police, he thought. But what if they don't find anything? I'll feel like a jerk—and, for sure, I'll end up having babysitters till I'm twenty.

So what do I do? Do I stay up here, scared out of my mind, or do I go down and find out what it is?

Luke made a decision.

"All right," he shouted. "I'm coming down."

He flicked on the light and stomped noisily down the rickety wooden stairs. In the stark glare of the single, naked bulb, the trunks and stacks of boxes cast eerie shadows on the dank stone walls. But that's all Luke saw. Just shadows.

Then his heart stopped. He heard the scratching again, coming from the window. Slowly, he turned toward the sound, fearful of what he'd see.

Holding his breath, he inched closer to the window and peered into the darkness. When he spotted the branch, it wasn't touching the glass. Then it swayed in the wind and scraped against the pane before bouncing back and away.

Luke let out his breath noisily. The lilac bush. Feeling foolish, he headed back upstairs. But he nearly jumped out of his skin when the telephone shrilled right beside him in the hall.

He grabbed the receiver on the second ring. "Hello."

Silence.

"Hello?"

More silence.

"Hey, is anybody there?'

Still more silence.

Luke shrugged as he hung up, then headed back into the living room. But he'd no sooner stuffed a warm nacho into his mouth than the phone rang again.

Jumping up, he knocked over the half-full can of cola on the table beside him. With one hand, he grabbed the can and righted it. With the other, he slapped a pile of paper napkins on the spill. Then he dashed back into the hall, shouting, "I'm coming. I'm coming."

He got to it on the sixth ring.

"Hello."

Silence.

"Who is this?" he shouted.

More silence.

"Hey, this isn't funny," he yelled, his voice cracking. Still more silence.

"Stop it, jerk," he screamed directly into the receiver, then slammed it down.

As he did, he remembered one of Stephanie's horror stories—about the babysitter who kept getting phone calls. When she answered, a deep, scary voice said only, "I'm coming to get you."

Terrified, she called the police. When they traced the call, they discovered it was coming from another line in the house. The thing on the other end of the line was upstairs all the time.

Luke looked up the stairs, then shook his head. "Thanks a lot, Stephanie," he muttered. "You're two hundred miles away and you're still scaring me to death."

Anyway, we don't have a separate line upstairs. Stop being an idiot, he told himself. It's probably just one of my so-called friends.

That's it. He felt better. The phone calls suddenly made sense.

Frankie had called earlier that afternoon to invite him over after dinner to watch a movie with him and Chris and Billy. He'd been tempted, but the thought of staying alone for the first time had won out. Besides, he wasn't all that crazy about Chris.

So he told Frankie he couldn't because his folks were going out and wouldn't be around to drive him home.

Telling Frankie this had obviously been a big mistake. Frankie must have told Billy and Chris why he hadn't joined them.

He could imagine the scene at the other end of the line—Chris dialing, and the other two smothering their laughter as he screamed, "Who's there?" He was guilty of making a few crank calls himself, so he knew that it could be fun. But not if you were on the receiving end. He'd learned that much tonight.

Still, now that he knew who was calling, he wasn't nervous anymore. He decided to turn the tables on the pranksters. He opened the junk drawer and dug out his sister's old lifeguard's whistle. Then he sat by the phone and waited, ready to answer their ring with one of his own.

He waited and waited. Nothing. Finally, he headed back to the living room to rescue his abandoned nachos. As he picked up the plate, he froze. He was sure he heard the scraping sound again, only this time it was coming from the kitchen. He moved quietly into the hall and listened. Nothing. He waited for what seemed like an eternity. Still nothing.

Stephanie, this is all your fault, he thought as he walked into the kitchen to pop the nachos back into the microwave for a quick warm-up. He saw the face just as he was pulling the plate out of the nuker.

Red eyes smoldering and long, sharp fangs bared in a horrible grimace, it was peering in the window. Then, as quickly as it had appeared, it was gone.

Nothing Stephanie had invented could have prepared him for this. Luke opened his mouth and screamed—and nearly dropped the plate. As he tried to juggle it, runny cheese and hot salsa splattered his hands. He dumped the plate on the counter and frantically wiped the burning splashes on his jeans.

He didn't want to, but he knew he had to look back at the window. All he saw was his own terrified face reflected in the dark glass.

Okay, okay, calm down, he urged himself. There was probably nothing there in the first place. It was my own reflection all along. But I don't look that bad. Nobody looks that bad, unless they're wearing a really gross mask.

Mask. That's it, he convinced himself. It was a mask, and I bet I know who was behind it. No wonder those guys never called back. How could they, if they were on their way over here to scare me some more?

This is Chris's dirty work, he thought. And he'll love telling everybody at school how I nearly wet my pants when I saw that mask. Boy, am I done for.

Suddenly, the scratching started again. It was coming from the living room.

Luke tiptoed out of the kitchen and down the hall. Tap, tap, tap. He reached around the doorway

to switch off the living-room light. The television filled the room with an eerie glow, but Luke wasn't afraid this time. He knew who was at the window and he intended to pay them back.

Tap, tap, scratch, scratch. The noise continued, louder now. It sounded like they were trying to get in. Stealthily, Luke slipped past the couch and around the coffee table. Then, very carefully, he moved over to the drapes covering the big double windows.

The sounds were coming from the window on the right. Slowly, Luke slipped his hand between the drapes and quietly released the lock. Then he carefully pulled back his hand and pressed himself against the wall. He opened the drapes a crack, then held his breath and waited.

It was very dark outside. He could barely make out the shadow slinking toward the window, but he couldn't miss the movement. He waited. The window inched open, then a dark shape reached under the frame and began to push upward.

At that moment, Luke struck. Throwing open the drape, he slammed the window down. He heard a terrible shriek, followed by a strangled whimper.

Horrified, Luke stepped back and let the drape fall into place. Oh no, he thought. What have I done? What if I broke his hand?

Frightened and confused, he backed away, waiting for Chris, Billy and Frankie to start yelling at him. But all he heard was more whimpering and a muffled scratching sound.

The ringing of the telephone shattered the silence. Hoping it was Mom or Dad, Luke dashed to answer. His hand shook as he picked up the receiver.

"Hello," he croaked.

"Hey, Luke. Listen, I'm sorry about the phone calls."

"Frankie? Is that you?"

"Yeah. Listen, it was Chris's idea, okay?"

"Frankie...where are you now?"

"I'm at home. Where do you think I am?"

"But, Chris and Billy are gone, right?"

"Nah, they're downstairs. I just came up to get some more chips and I thought I'd let you know it was us, just in case you hadn't figured it out yet. Listen. I gotta go. I'll call you tomorrow."

"Wait, Frankie, don't hang up," Luke whispered hoarsely, but he was too late. The line was dead.

Slowly, he replaced the receiver. Then he turned and stared wide-eyed into the shadows of the living room. Weak with fear, he slumped against the post at the bottom of the stairs.

Stay calm, he ordered, but his body wasn't listening. His heart felt like a jackhammer and the blood pounded in his head. Stop it. Stop it, he commanded. Calm down and call Mom and Dad.

He reached for the phone, then froze. The number was stuck on the fridge. And the living-room window was still unlocked. His skin turned to goose flesh. Whatever was out there might get in while he was in the kitchen.

Terrified, Luke put down the receiver and looked around for a weapon. His baseball bat was leaning against the wall. Gripping it in both hands, he stepped into the living room and moved quickly to the window. Summoning his last ounce of courage, he yanked the drapes open and jumped back, ready to lash out with the bat.

Seeing nothing, he banged the lock back into place. With a sigh of relief, he reached over to draw the drapes again. As he did, his hand brushed something wet and slimy.

Recoiling, Luke dropped the bat and staggered into the hall. He held up his hand. Green slime dripped down his arm.

Luke's knees turned to jelly and he collapsed in a heap on the floor.

That's where his parents found him ten minutes later, still wiping his hand on his jeans and muttering, "This is your fault, Stephanie. Your fault. No fair."

Spellbound

When the old car pulling a battered silver trailer chugged slowly up the long hill to the Oakley house that day in mid-October, it took about five minutes for the news to get around town. The rundown house had been empty for so long that everyone said it was haunted. Now, the whole town was curious to know who on earth would move in—and why.

Joey Dean and Marty Kane took it upon themselves to be the first to find out. Quietly, the two boys worked their way up the rutted lane. Crouching low behind the overgrown bushes that were threatening to take over the weed-choked yard, they stole to the rear of the house and hid beside a ramshackle shed.

From there, they had a clear view of the trailer and the weatherbeaten porch that clung precariously to the back of the house. Undetected, they watched the comings and goings of three people—a man, a woman, and a girl—as they shifted boxes, bags and a few suitcases into the house.

"So, they really are moving in," Joey whispered, "but who'd want to live here?"

"Yeah, this place gives me the major creeps," Marty whispered back. "And so do they, right?" he added.

Joey looked at the strangers. They were standing on the porch, gazing out across the hill at the deep rose and purple of a darkening autumn sky. The girl, her face eerily pale in the fading light, was wearing a long black skirt sprinkled with yellow stars. The woman had on a colorful poncho and the man's shoulder-length hair hung down from under a black hat with a wide, bent brim.

Joey shrugged. Marty was right. They did look a little strange.

"Well, they're...different," he said noncommittally.

"The guy's got long hair. My dad says that's how you can spot weirdos a mile away. And look at that skirt. They must be related to the Addams family." Marty giggled at his own joke.

Suddenly, the girl called out, "Hey, Dad. Look."

"It's a bit late in the year for that fellow to be out," the man said, as the girl picked up what looked like a twisting, dancing piece of rope. "He must have found a warm spot here under the steps."

"See that?" Marty hissed and elbowed Joey in the ribs. "They like snakes. For sure, they're going to..."

He stopped in mid-sentence, interrupted by a rustling in the bushes behind them. Startled, the two boys turned. When the black-and-white shape emerged, Marty bolted.

As his friend crashed noisily through the undergrowth, Joey heard the man call out, "Who's there?"

Joey hesitated just long enough to see the skunk's tail shoot up like a flag, then he took off after Marty.

He caught up with him at the bottom of the hill.

"That was close," Marty panted. "It nearly got us."

"Well, it wouldn't have done anything if you'd just stayed still," Joey protested.

"Says who?" Marty snarled.

Says me, Joey thought, but he knew better than to argue with Marty. Marty was a pretty good friend—as long as he got his own way. Worried that he might have already crossed the line, Joey fell in behind him without saying another word.

They were both out of breath when they reached the Burger Barn, but that didn't stop

Marty. He gasped dramatically as he burst through the doors, staggering and clutching his chest as if he'd just outraced a slavering wolf.

"What's with you?" Paula Stroud called.

That was the only cue Marty needed. As Paula and the other kids gathered round, he launched into his tale. The strangers on the porch became snake-charming, spell-casting, blood-sucking, shrieking maniacs who had pursued the two boys down the hill.

Joey enjoyed the story, too, though he objected feebly when Marty reported that the girl had tried to bite off the snake's head. But no one paid any attention, anyway. And when he tried to interrupt again, Marty warned him off with a look that said, Keep your mouth shut.

"We were lucky to get away," Marty finished, his face flushed. He was playing up to every squeal of horror from his audience.

Over the weekend, Marty's tale spread quickly—and more rumors were added with each retelling. By the time Monday morning rolled around, the stage was set.

When the girl and her mother walked through the schoolyard gate, the whispering and pointing started immediately.

Marty wasted no time. Separating himself from the group that had gathered round him, he swaggered over to the pair. "Whatcha got in the bag—snake heads?"

The girl looked puzzled. She stared at Marty, then down at her bag, a green cloth carry-all with a rainbow stitched across the front.

"Books and pens," she said quietly, pulling a dog-eared notebook out of the bag. "And my lunch," she added, patting a bulge in the bag. Then she smiled and, with her mother, continued walking into the school.

Watching them climb the stairs, Joey felt a pang of guilt. Once again, though, he hid behind his silence. Why, he wondered, do I let Marty drag me into stuff like this? Because Marty rules, that's why. What he says, goes.

The principal showed up later that morning with Lilith Carsons in tow. When he invited her to introduce herself to the class, a stony silence greeted her.

Nervously, Lilith began to explain that her family had come from New Mexico, that she loved reading and animals, and that her parents had been hired by an Oakley heir to spend the next year repairing and restoring the old house. Her eyes lit up when she described how wonderful it would look.

As she spoke, some of the kids began directing skeptical glances at Marty. By the time she finished, he'd lost a few believers. His description just didn't match the person standing before them.

But this didn't stop him. In fact, it was like waving a red flag in front of a bull. There was no way Marty was going to let the truth get in the way of a great story.

"Who ever heard of a name like Lilith?" he asked in a stage whisper as she passed his desk.

The giggles that followed ended abruptly when she turned, looked him straight in the eye, and said simply, "My mother and father. That's two. And now you make three."

Marty blinked and turned away instantly, as if a flash bulb had just popped in his face.

But as Lilith continued walking, he recovered. Determined not to give up his advantage, he grabbed his head and rolled noisily out of his chair, groaning, "The evil eye. She got me with the evil eye."

Over the next few days, Marty escalated his campaign of lies. When Lilith carefully picked up a small spider in the lunchroom and put it gently out the window, he told everyone within earshot that he'd seen a huge, hairy black one poking out of her bag.

"She collects them for spells," he declared.

When she rescued an injured field mouse from the ditch near the school one afternoon and started home with it, Marty pointed out to anyone who would listen that she was taking it home to feed the bats.

"What bats? Where?" Paula squirmed.

"The ones she keeps in the shed," Marty ad-libbed.

"No kidding," Gordon Petrie piped up.

"Marty," Joey finally spoke up, "you're nuts."

Marty's eyes flashed. He grabbed Joey by the arm and pulled him to one side. "What do you think you're doing, Joey?"

"Marty, you know you're spreading garbage."

"Oh yeah? What makes you so sure, Joey?"

"Marty, I was there that first day, remember. I know what really happened."

"So?"

"So, if you don't stop, I'm going to tell everybody the truth—that we took off because we saw a skunk and...," Joey stopped short, suddenly realizing what he was doing. He waited for Marty's counterattack, but it didn't come.

Marty just stared. "I don't believe this. She's got just about everybody fooled—including you." He turned abruptly and stormed away.

"I'm right about her. You'll see," he shouted over his shoulder.

Joey was confused. Marty might be pushy sometimes—well, actually, most of the time—but he isn't stupid, he thought. He's sure acting stupid about Lilith, though. People are starting to laugh at him, not her.

She's definitely getting to Marty. But, he admitted, maybe she's getting to me, too. Isn't it because of her that I finally stood up to Marty?

Joey frowned. Could there really be something different...something strange...about Lilith? He shook his head, banishing the thought.

But the next day, thoughts of spells and spooks and goblins were on everyone's mind, Joey's included. It was Halloween and, around town, the excitement was building. In an attempt to patch things up with Marty, Joey called him to see if they'd be trick-or-treating together as usual. Marty turned him down flat, saying he had better things to do that night.

Joey didn't like the sound of this. What's Marty up to? he wondered. Halloween could be the perfect camouflage for someone looking for trouble. And if Marty was planning something nasty, Lilith was probably his target.

Joey made a quick decision. When dusk fell and the orange pumpkins began to flicker and glow, he was already in place. From his hiding spot across the street at the bottom of the Oakley lane, he watched as a solitary jack-o-lantern, glowing brightly, was perched on the gatepost. He felt sure its invitation would be ignored. No one was likely to test the theory that the house was haunted, especially not on Halloween.

But Joey did see Lilith come down the lane. Once again, she was wearing the flowing black skirt covered in stars. A mask of feathers hid her face and a shimmering web-like shawl covered her shoulders.

Joey also saw the werewolf, which had been lurking in the shelter of some bushes, slip out of the darkness and start to follow her. Marty had worn the same werewolf costume last year and the year before.

I was right, Joey thought as the two figures passed him. He's after her. But what is he going to do? Grabbing the hem of the sheet that covered him from head to toe, he fell into step a safe distance behind them.

The strange, silent parade of three wound up and down the dimly lit streets. Lilith's bag grew heavier at each stop, but Marty's and Joey's stayed empty. Neither wanted to lose track of his quarry.

Just before Lilith turned back onto Main Street, Marty made his move. He increased his pace and caught up to Lilith in the shadows behind the Burger Barn. He ran up behind her, growling and snarling, and snatched her bag. Then he disappeared around the corner.

Joey was too far behind to do anything. He tried to catch up, but his legs tangled in the sheet. When he finally staggered up to Lilith, she was just standing there slipping the ends of her filmy shawl through her fingers.

"It's me. Joey," he blurted. "Are you all right?"

"Yeah. I'm fine."

"I'll get it back," he offered, struggling to pull off the sheet. "Hold this," he said, thrusting his bag and the sheet into Lilith's startled hands. "I'll be right back."

"Joey, you don't have to...," Lilith began, but Joey was already turning the corner. He heard Marty before he saw him. His strangled scream pierced the night air.

Marty had pulled off his mask and was standing beside the bench in front of the post office. Lilith's bag lay in a crumpled heap at his feet. His face was contorted in horror and, suddenly, he started flailing wildly at his costume.

Joey stopped dead, then jumped back. The bench—and the pavement beneath it—was covered with every creepy-crawly imaginable. Snakes slithered, spiders scuttled, and bugs scattered in all directions, some of them clinging to the fur of Marty's costume. Out of the darkness, bats suddenly swooped around his head. Trying to duck and brush away the creatures at the same

time, Marty looked like he was doing some kind of crazy dance.

Lilith slipped through the small crowd that had gathered to witness the scene and stood next to Joey. When Marty saw her, he froze.

"Get her away from me," he shouted frantically. "She did it. She did it."

"Did what?" Joey asked. "Let you steal her bag, then pretend this stuff was in it?"

"How do you know that I stole...?" Marty stopped. "But wait, that means you saw. You saw what happened. You know what she did."

"I don't know what you're talking about," Joey said, walking away.

He felt the tug on his arm halfway up the street. It was Lilith. She'd taken off her mask. It was dangling on her wrist from a thin white elastic. As the feathers moved, they looked like a strange bird getting ready to take flight.

"You forgot these," Lilith said, holding out his sheet and bag. The bag was full.

Joey took the sheet and started to reach for the bag, then pulled back his hand. He looked uncomfortably at Lilith, remembering what had happened to Marty.

"Don't worry. It's okay," she smiled knowingly.

Joey took the bag. Carefully, he opened it and reached in. Nothing crawled up his arm. Nothing slithered through his fingers. In fact, the bag was full of familiar shapes.

Joey pulled out two peanut butter cups.

"Want one?" he asked.

"Thanks," she said, taking one. "They're my favorites."

"Mine too."

"I know," Lilith said quietly.